꿈을 찾는
삶의 영어

꿈을 찾는 삶의 영어

초판 1쇄 발행 2022년 6월 20일

지은이 정은혜
펴낸이 장현수
펴낸곳 메이킹북스
출판등록 제 2019-000010호

디자인 비오프디
편집 박단비
교정 강인영
마케팅 장윤정

주소 서울특별시 구로구 경인로 661, 핀포인트타워 912-914호
전화 02-2135-5086
팩스 02-2135-5087
이메일 making_books@naver.com
홈페이지 www.makingbooks.co.kr

ISBN 979-11-6791-174-2(03740)
값 14,900원

ⓒ 정은혜 2022 Printed in Korea

잘못된 책은 구입하신 곳에서 바꾸어 드립니다.
이 책의 전부 또는 일부 내용을 재사용하려면 사전에 저작권자와 펴낸곳의 동의를 받아야 합니다.

홈페이지 바로가기

메이킹북스는 저자님의 소중한 투고 원고를 기다립니다.
출간에 대한 관심이 있으신 분은 making_books@naver.com으로 보내 주세요.

꿈을 찾는 삶의 영어

정은혜 지음

메이킹북스

저자 소개

정은혜(Scarlett)

캐나다 토론토 조지브라운 대학(George Brown College)을 졸업하였다. 캐나다 토론토에서 TESOL, 한국에서 OPIC AL을 취득 후 대치 어학원에서는 아이들을, 강남 성인어학원에서는 성인들을 대상으로 비즈니스 영어, OPIC을 가르쳤으며 건대 YBM에서 성인을 대상으로 '술술 써지는 영작문' 강의를 한 경험이 있다.

왜 영어였을까? 인생을 관통하는 단 한 권의 책을 만난 후 영어는 저자의 삶을 완전히 바꿔놓았다. 저자는 고등학교 3학년까지 파닉스와 형용사, 동사도 구분하지 못할 정도로 기본기가 없었다. 영어를 잘하지도, 하려고 하지도 않았던 그녀는 그 책을 만남으로써 인생을 바꾸게 되었다.

"나 같은 애도 하면 된다." 호기로운 다짐이었다. 반 아이들은 그녀가 공부한다는 것을 매우 신기해하고 의아해했다.

그로부터 1년 반 뒤 그녀는 한국에서 영어로 성인 과외를 시작한다. 공부하는 방법조차 모르던 저자가 1년이라는 시간 뒤에 누군가를 가르칠 수 있었던 건 단 하나, 마음에 품은 독기와 열정이었다.

영어를 14시간 이상 공부하며 "나 같은 애도 하면 된다"라는 다짐은 "나도 하면 할 수 있구나"라는 배움으로 남았다. 아무것도 모르던 상태로 시작했던 저자는 이제 학습 장애와 시작을 어려워하는 사람들을 위해 그들의 삶에 선한 영향을 줄 수 있는 영어 교육계에 발을 들이게 된다. 저자의 기적을 모든 사람에게 나누기 위해, 기적은 결코 기적이 아닌 노력으로 일어날 수 있음을 모두에게 증명하기 위해 오늘도 영어를 가르친다.

삶은 자기 계발의 도화지라고 생각한다. 영어 스피킹을 시작하기 겁나는 사람, 아직 하고 싶은 말을 제대로 하지 못하는 사람들을 위해 자기 계발서와 스피킹을 접목한 이 책을 썼다. 하고 싶은 말을 할 수 있다는 것, 그것에서부터 삶의 도화지에 한 획을 그을 수 있다고 확신한 저자의 삶이 담겨 있다.

이 책은 Scarlett이라는 영어 강사(친구)인 그녀를 알아가며 에세이를 읽듯 영어 회화를 배울 수 있는 신선한 책이다.

Table of Contents

I. 스칼렛 알아가기
Getting to Know Scarlett 초급: **Beginner** 11

1. 만나서 반가워요: 친구 되기
   Nice to Meet You!: Becoming a Friend 초급 12
   ※ 인사 / 대답하기 : Greeting / Answering 12

2. 취미가 뭐예요?:
   상대를 알아 갈 때 가장 많이 묻는 말 14
   ※ 취미 물어보기 14

3. 스트레스 받을 때 주로 뭐해요?
   What do you do when you get stressed? 21
   ※ 남자친구와 놀아요 I go see my boyfriend. 21
   ※ 술 마셔요 I drink. 22
   ※ 영화 봐요 I watch movies. 23
   ※ 친구랑 수다 떨어요 I chat with my friends. 23
   ※ 교육에 관심이 많아요 I'm interested in education. 23

4. 시간 날 때 주로 뭐해요?
What do you do in your free time? ... 25

- 자기 계발하기 Self-improvement ... 25
- 일찍 일어나기 Get up early ... 26
- 나의 경력 쌓기 Build up your career ... 27
- 경력과 관련된 자격증 따기
  I enjoy obtaining certifications that are related to my job. ... 28
- 운동하기 Work out: Exercise: Engage in physical activities ... 31
- 영어 배우기 Learning English ... 31
- 독서하기 Reading books ... 32

II. 스칼렛 더 자세히 알아가기 ... 33

1. 왜 그것들을 하세요?
Why do you like doing those activities? 중급/중상급 ... 34

- 남자친구란... A boyfriend is... ... 34
- 술이란... Drinking is... ... 39
- 친구랑 수다를 떠는 건... Chatting with friends is ... 41
- 나의 경력 발전시키는 건... Building your career ... 44
- 경력과 관련된 자격증 따기
  Obtaining certifications relating to my job ... 47
- 영화 보는 건... Watching movies is... ... 49
- 공부란... Studying is important because... ... 52

2. 자기계발이란...
Self-improvement is... ... 54

- 일찍 일어나기 Getting up early ... 54

- ※ 운동하기... Exercising is...   57
- ※ 영어를 배우는 건... Studying English is...   61
- ※ 독서하는 것은... Reading book is...   64

3. 스트레스를 주로 언제 받아요?
When do you usually get stressed?   67

- ※ 직장/사회생활 Work & Social Life   67
- ※ 친구 Friends   70
- ※ 가족 Family   73
- ※ 취업 Looking for a Job   74
- ※ 성공 Success   76

4. 평상시 일상 Daily routine   80

- ※ 현재의 내 일상 My Daily Routine   80
- ※ 내 과거의 일상 My Past Routine   84
- ※ 내가 바라는 미래의 일상 My Future Routine   86

III. 스칼렛의 삶 이야기
Scarlett's Life Story   91

1. When was a time when you were the happiest?
넌 가장 행복했을 때가 언제야?   92

- ※ 스칼렛의 삶 이야기 Scarlett's Life Story   95

IV. 넌 목표와 꿈이 뭐야?
What are your goals and dreams?   103

    1. 내 꿈과 목표는... My dreams and goals are...   104

V. 뜬금없지만 감사함으로 마무리하기! J   107

VI. 영어를 배우려면
이분들과 이런 기능들을 이용하자!   129

스칼렛을 같이 알아보러 가봅시다!
Let's get to know Scarlett together!

I

스칼렛 알아가기
Getting to Know Scarlett

초급: Beginner

1. 만나서 반가워요: 친구 되기
Nice to Meet You!: Becoming a Friend 초급

❋ **인사/대답하기: Greeting / Answering**

Hi! I'm Scarlett! Nice to meet you.
안녕하세요, 저는 스칼렛이에요! 만나서 반가워요!

(저도) 만나서 반가워요
1. I'm _____, it's nice to meet you, too!
2. I'm _____, it is a pleasure to meet you!
3. I'm _____, it is a delight to meet you.

* 문법 포인트

1. 이것만은 꼭 기억하자.
영어 문장을 만들 때는 **주어 + 동사**가 필요하다.
주어 뒤 **동사/형용사/명사** 어떤 형태의 단어가 나오느냐에 따라 be 동사(am, is, are 등 중에)의 필요성 을 판단할 수 있다.
주어 + 일반 동사가 나올 경우에는 be 동사가 들어가지 않는다.
만약 주어 + 형용사나 명사가 나오면 주어 바로 뒤 be 동사가 나오게 된다.

2. **It   is   nice** to meet you too!
주어(대명사 단수) is= be동사(단수) ... 형용사
가주어인(뜻이 없는 가짜 주어) It을 쓰고 반갑다고 말할 때 원하는 형용사들을 사용하여 문장들을 응용할 수 있다.

인사할 때 많이 쓰이는 형용사

good - 좋은   **pleasure** - 기쁨, 즐거움   **nice** - 좋은, 즐거운, 멋진
happy - 행복한   **delight** - 기쁨   **lovely** - 사랑스러운, 훌륭한, 아주 좋은
glad - 기쁜, 반가운 등...

> 예 It is **형용사(adjective)** to meet you.

1. It is good to meet you.
2. It is nice to meet you.
3. It is lovely to meet you. (주로 미국보단 영국이나 호주에서 많이 쓰인다.)
4. I'm glad to meet you.
5. I'm happy to meet you.

위 단어 4, 5번 glad와 happy는 사람의 감정에 대해 쓰는 표현이기 때문에 'it's'보다는 'I am'으로 시작하는 게 맞다.

표현들 중 감정을 넣어 연기자가 된 것처럼 소리 내어 5번 내뱉어 보고 체크해 봅시다.

1st	2nd	3rd	4th	5th

2. 취미가 뭐예요?: 상대를 알아 갈 때 가장 많이 묻는 말

❋ 취미 물어보기

1. What are your hobbies?
   (당신은) 취미(들이) 뭐예요?
2. What do you usually do for fun?
   (당신은) 재미로 하는 게 주로 뭐예요? = 심심할 때 주로 뭐하세요?
3. What do you normally do when you have free time?
   (당신은) 시간 날 때 주로 뭐하세요?

* 문법 포인트

> 육하원칙 = 5W1H
> Questions = Who, What, Where, When, Why, How

육하원칙 뒤에 나올 핵심 단어가 어떤 성질인지에 따라 문장 구조가 바뀐다.
What are your hobbies? ⇒ 문장의 핵심단어 취미'들'(복수= 명사)이기에 What 뒤 의문문에서는 is가 아니라 are이 나온다.
과거가 아닌 평소 반복적으로 하는 취미를 묻고 있으니 현재형으로 are를 사용해 주었다.
2, 3번 문장의 핵심 단어는 'do'이다. do(하다) = 일반 동사이고 주어는 You(너)이기 때문에(일반 동사를 사용한 의문문은 Did, does, do로 시작한다) 3인칭에 쓰이는 Does가 아닌 Do가 사용되었다.

* For : 위해 재미로, 즐거움을 위해

* 연습하기! (물어보기)

> **예** What do you do for fun?
> 너는 재미로 뭘 해? = 당신은 심심할 때 뭐해요?

What do you do 뒤를 다양하게 연결시키기!

> **What do you do** when you are free?
> 시간 날 때는 뭐해요?
> **What do you do** when you get bored?
> 심심할 때는 뭐해요?

여기에 빈도 부사도 추가하면 문장이 풍성해진다.

> What do you **usually** do when you have plenty of time?
> 시간이 많을 때 **대개** 뭐해요?
> What do you **normally** do when you don't go to work?
> 출근하지 않을 때 **일반적**으로 뭐하세요?

표현들 중 감정을 넣어 연기자가 된 것처럼 소리 내어 5번 내뱉어 보고 체크해 봅시다.

1st	2nd	3rd	4th	5th

* 보너스 연습!

빈 칸을 채워 나의 새 친구에게 질문을 만들어 봅시다.

1. What do you usually do _____?
2. What do you _____?
3. What _____?
4. _____?
5. _____?

* **연습하기 (대답하기)**

My hobbies are 동명사.	→ 내 취미들은 **동명사** 하는 것이야.
만들어 보기	
I usually 동사 for fun.	→ 나는 주로 심심할 때 **동사**를 해.
만들어 보기	
I normally 동사 when I have time.	→ 저는 주로 시간이 날 때면 **동사**를 해요.
만들어 보기	
I enjoy + 동명사.	→ 저는 **동명사** 하는 것을 즐겨요.
만들어 보기	
I love + 동명사.	→ 저는 **동명사** 하는 것을 매우 좋아해요.
만들어 보기	
I like to + 동사.	→ 저는 **동사** 하는 것을 좋아해요.
만들어 보기	
I'm interested in 동명사 or 명사.	→ 저는 **동명사 혹은 명사**에 관심이 있어요.
만들어 보기	

표현들 중 감정을 넣어 연기자가 된 것처럼 소리 내어 5번 내뱉어 보고 체크해 봅시다.

1st	2nd	3rd	4th	5th

* **문법 포인트와 예문**

명사 (My hobby / hobbies) be 동사

예 My hobby is ....
　　My hobbie**s** are ...

주어가 단수인지 복수인지 생각하며 말하기

내가 하는 것에 대해 말할 때
I usually 동사 for fun. 나는 주로 심심할 때(재미로) 동사를 해.

> 예문

I usually(주로) watch(동사: 보다) TV(목적어를: TV를).
나는 주로 TV를 봐요.
I usually go to the gym.
나는 주로 헬스장에 가요.
I usually meet my friends.
나는 주로 친구들을 만나요.
I usually shop online using my phone.
I usually do online-shopping using my phone.
I shop online using my phone.
나는 주로 휴대폰을 사용해서 쇼핑을 해요. = 나는 휴대폰으로 쇼핑을 해요.

저는 주로 시간이 날 때면 **동사**를 해요.
I normally 동사 when I have time

> 예문

I normally read books when I have time.
나는 주로 내가 시간이 있을 때 책을 읽어요.
I normally study English when I have time.
나는 주로 내가 시간이 있을 때 영어를 공부해요.
I normally talk with my friends on the phone.
나는 주로 내가 시간이 있을 때 친구랑 통화해요.

주어진 단어로 문장 만들어 보기

빈도 부사: usually, normally, typically, generally

1. I_____.
2. She_____.
3. He_____.
4. Scarlett_____.
5. They _____.

표현들 중 감정을 넣어 연기자가 된 것처럼 소리 내어 5번 내뱉어 보고 체크해 봅시다.

1st	2nd	3rd	4th	5th

I enjoy + 동명사.
저는 (동명사)하는 것을 즐겨요.

예문

I enjoy going to the movies.
저는 영화 보러 가는 것을 즐겨요.
I enjoy playing computer games.
저는 컴퓨터 게임을 하는 것을 즐겨요.
I enjoy binge-watching my favorite TV shows.
저는 내가 좋아하는 TV 프로그램들을 정주행하는 것을 즐겨요.

* Binge-watch = 정주행하다   * binge- 몰아서 하다

위 예문 보고 문장 만들어 보기
1. I_____.
2. She_____.
3. He_____.
4. Scarlett_____.
5. They _____.

표현들 중 감정을 넣어 연기자가 된 것처럼 소리 내어 5번 내뱉어 보고 체크해 봅시다.

1st	2nd	3rd	4th	5th

꿈을 찾는 **삶의 영어**

> I like to + 동사
> 저는 (동사)하는 것을 좋아해요.

🔷 예문

I like to watch TV shows all at once.
TV 프로그램 정주행하는 것을 좋아해요.
I like to sleep in on the weekends as much as I can.
주말에는 내가 할 수 있는 한 잠을 몰아서 자는 것을 좋아해요.
He likes binge watching Netflix at home.
(3인칭 주어로 바꿔보기!) 그는 집에서 넷플릭스 정주행하는 것을 좋아해요.
She likes binge shopping on the Black Friday.
그녀는 블랙프라이데이 때 쇼핑을 몰아서 하는 것을 좋아해요.
I'm binge watching my favorite K-dramas right now.
나는 지금 내가 가장 좋아하는 한류 드라마들을 몰아서 보고 있어.
My friend is binge cleaning the house at the moment.
내 친구는 지금 집을 몰아서 치우고 있어.

　　　　　　　　　　　　* Binge- 혼자서는 잘 쓰이지 않는 단어
　　실제로 binge는 동사이긴 하지만 미국인들은 binge+ 동사+ing 를 추가해서 쓴다.

I like to go window shopping.
난 아이쇼핑하는 것을 좋아해요.
I like to dine at new restaurants.
난 새로운 식당들을 탐험 하는 것을 좋아해요.
I like to try to go to a book store.
난 서점 가는 것을 좋아해요.

　　　　　　　　　　　　　* dine out (숙어) = 외식을 하다
　　　　　　　　　　　　　* dine (동사) = 근사한 식사를 하다

I'm interested in 동명사 or 명사.
저는 (동명사 혹은 명사)에 관심이 있어요.

예문

I'm interested in learning new languages.
전 새로운 언어들을 배우는 것을 좋아해요.
I'm interested in psychology.
전 심리학에 관심이 있어요.
I'm interested in playing the guitar.
저는 기타 치는 것에 관심 있어요.

위 예문 보고 문장 만들어 보기

1. I_____.
2. She_____.
3. He_____.
4. Scarlett_____.
5. They _____.

표현들 중 감정을 넣어 연기자가 된 것처럼 소리 내어 5번 내뱉어 보고 체크해 봅시다.

1st	2nd	3rd	4th	5th

3. 스트레스 받을 때 주로 뭐해요?
What do you do when you get stressed?

※ 남자친구와 놀아요 I go see my boyfriend

* I **go to see** my boyfriend. = 나는 남자친구를 보러 간다.
  (로봇 같은 말투, 쓰이지 않는 말투)
* I **go see** my boyfriend. = 나는 남자친구 보러 가.
  두 동사가 나와서 이런 식으로도 쓰인다

> 예) Go sleep! - 가서 자!
> Go do your homework! – 가서 숙제 해!
> Go eat – 밥 먹어!
> Go read! – 책 읽으세요!

My hobbies are watching movies with my boyfriend.
남자친구랑 영화를 봐요.
I love to drink with my boyfriend.
남자친구와 같이 술을 마셔요
I enjoy walk**ing** around my neighborhood with my boyfriend.
남자친구와 같이 동네 산책을 해요.
I normally watch TV shows with my boyfriend on Netflix.
남자친구와 같이 넷플릭스 프로그램을 봐요.

* 스칼렛의 설명 시간
Hang out – play ← 는 주로 어린 아이들이 쓰는 단어!
7살 이전 아이들이 소꿉장난 같은 놀이를 할 때 쓰이고 어른들은 성적인 용어에서도 쓰이니 주의하기!
Hang out은 어느 정도 나이를 먹은 청소년 어른들이 '놀다, 어울려 놀다'를 쓰고 싶을 때 쓸 수 있는 단어이다.

많이들 'drink alcohol'이라고 하는데 굳이 원어민들은 "오늘 알코올 마실 거야!"라고 하지 않고 '오늘 (술) 마시자!'라는 뉘앙스로 뒤에 alcohol을 붙이지 않고 사용한다.
예 Let's go for a drink! – 오늘 한잔하자!

* 솔로일 경우 When you are a single.
Where is my boyfriend?
내 남친은 어디에 있는 것인가...?
혹은 'DTA'라는 표현도 있다.
"Don't Trust Anybody."
이 표현은 한 레슬링 선수의 슬로건이었는데 직역하면 "아무도 믿지 마라"라는 뜻이지만 미국에서는 '어차피 인생은 혼자다'라는 의미로 쓰인다.
 * 구글에 Don't trust anybody meme를 검색해 보면 다양한 사진들이 많이 나온다.

❋ 술 마셔요 I drink

When I get stressed, I relieve them by drinking **beer.**
(밑줄 친 부분에 맥주를 제외한 좋아하는 음료, 술을 넣을 수 있다.
예 vodka, cocktails, cider...)

* 스칼렛의 설명과 예문
When I get stressed, I relieve them by drinking.
난 스트레스 받을 때 술 마시면서 스트레스 풀어요.
When I get stressed, I relieve them by drinking vodka.
난 스트레스 받을 때 보드카를 마시면서 스트레스 풀어요.
 * cider 한국에서는 사이다를 영어로 간혹 알고 쓰는 경우도 있는데 서양에서 cider는 주로 사과나 과일로 만든 알코올이 들어간 달달한 술을 말한다.

✢ 영화 봐요 I watch movies

I like watching movies such as romance (comedies, or any genre)
　　　　　　　　　　　　　　　　　　　좋아하는 장르 넣기
예) comedies, thrillers, science fiction, mystery, horror, fantasy, action 등

✢ 친구랑 수다 떨어요 I chat with my friends

저는 친구랑 전화를 자주 해요.
I often talk on the phone with my friends.
저는 친구들을 볼 때마다 수다를 떨어요.
I chat with my friends whenever I see them.

다른 비슷한 예문

저는 휴식(커피 마실) 시간 동안 동료들과 수다를 떨어요.
I chat with my coworkers during the coffee breaks.
저는 할머니 집에 가면 할머니랑 수다를 떠는 것을 좋아해요.
I like to chat it up with my grandma when I visit her place.

　　　　　　　　　　　　　　　　　　　* chat it up 수다를 떨다

✽ 스칼렛의 설명 시간
Talk on the phone
전화한다 call을 쓰는 것은 직접 전화를 거는 느낌으로 통화 한다고 하면 Talk on the phone을 자주 쓴다.
여기서 call 뒤에 전치사를 쓰지 않는 것에 주의한다. 노래나 미드에서 call me! 를 자주 들어 봤을 것이다. Call 뒤에는 보통 바로 목적어가 나온다.

✢ 교육에 관심이 많아요 I'm interested in education

저는 교육을 배우는 것을 즐기고 관심 있어 해요.
I'm interested in and enjoy learning about education.
저는 심리학을 배우는 것을 즐기고 관심 있어 해요.
I'm interested in and enjoy learning about psychology.

* **문법 포인트**

Be + interested in + 명사 혹은 동명사를 쓰면 다양한 문장들을 만들 수 있다.

* **나만의 도화지 채워 넣기**

What are you interested in these days?
(요즘 뭐에 관심이 있으신가요?)
대답하기 :
1. I'm interested in _____.
2.
3.
4.
5.

내가 작문한 문장을 소리 내서 읽어 봅시다.

1st	2nd	3rd	4th	5th

4. 시간 날 때 주로 뭐해요?
What do you do in your free time?

❋ 자기 계발하기 | Self-improvement

I enjoy doing self-improvement activities such as...
나는 자기 계발하는 활동을 하는 것을 좋아해요. 가령...
I enjoy being the best version of myself.
저는 저의 최고의 버전(모습)으로 살아가는 걸 즐깁니다.
I'm interested in personal growth, self-development, and becoming more efficient and effective.
저는 저를 성장시키는 것, 자기 계발, 내 자신이 더 효율적이고 효과적이게 되는 것에 관심이 많아요.

* 문법 포인트

Enjoy(동사: 즐기다) + 동사가 또 나올 경우에는 뒤에 동사에 (ing) 추가하기!
위에서의 예시들과 같이 응용할 수 있다.

> Love 와 like는 두 개의 동사를 사용해야 할 때
> 1. I like to
> 2. I like + ing 둘 다 올 수 있다.
> Like는 to 부정사, 동명사 둘 다 될 수 있다.

* 연습하기

What do you do in your free time?
1. I enjoy
2. I love
3. I'm interested in
4. I like
5. I normally

내가 시간 날 때 주로 하는 일에 대한 문장을 만든 후 소리 내서 읽어 봅시다.

1st	2nd	3rd	4th	5th

❈ 일찍 일어나기 Get up early

I enjoy getting up early in the morning.
저는 아침 일찍 일어나는 것을 즐겨요.
I enjoy waking up early.
저는 일찍 일어나는 것을 즐겨요.

차이점

Get up
평상시에 "일어나, 일어나." 이런 느낌

Wake up
긴박한 상황에 빨리 깨울 때나 "야! 늦었어! 일어나!", "정신 차려!"로도 쓰인다.
"정신 차려!(Pull yourself together!)"도 쓰인다. (매우 강한 어조)

* 스칼렛의 설명 시간

Early in the morning 이른 아침
그렇다면 늦은 저녁, 초저녁, 늦은 아침은?
늦은 저녁 – late-night / late evening
초저녁 – early evening
늦은 아침 – late morning
I enjoy getting up early in the morning.
노란 부분에 다른 시점을 넣어 여러 가지 문장을 만들 수 있다.

✤ 나의 경력 쌓기 Build up your career

I love to build up my career.
저는 제 경력을 쌓는 것을 좋아해요.
I feel fulfilled from building up rapport with my coworkers.
나는 직장 동료들과 돈독한 관계를 만드는 것에서 성취감을 느껴요.

* rapport – 좋은 돈독한 관계

* 스칼렛의 설명 시간
Fulfilled, accomplished, satisfied + content의 차이점이 뭘까?

Fulfilled(동사, 형용사): 무엇을 이루어 낸 후 내가 느끼는(성취감), 속 시원함, 후련함이 크다!의 의미
(예시: 돌탑을 쌓던 한 할아버지가 마지막 하나를 완성했을 때)

 예문
The old man has **fulfilled** his life's destiny when he put the last piece of rock on his tower of rocks.
돌탑을 완성하고 나서 후련함을 느꼈다. (동사)
Scarlett is feeling **fulfilled** after finishing her book.
스칼렛은 그 책을 끝낸 후 후련함을 느꼈다. (형용사)

Accomplished: 내가 무엇을 이루어 내었다는(성취감), 무엇을 이루어 내어서 그것이 자랑스럽다.

 예문
I've **accomplished** a lot today. (동사 격)
오늘 해낸 일이 많다.
I'm an **accomplished** scientist. (형용사 격)
나는 이루어 낸 것이 많은 과학자이다.

Satisfied: '만족한(형용사: 상태)'이라는 뜻으로 웬만한 긍정적인 문장에는 다 쓸 수 있는 단어.
I'm so **satisfied** with this hamburger that I ordered.
난 내가 주문한 이 햄버거에 완전 만족해.
I'm so **satisfied** with my accomplishment!

난 내 업적에 완전 만족해!
I'm so **satisfied** with your performance!
너의 수행 능력에 완전 만족해! (너 일 잘하는구나!)

* Fulfilled 는 accomplished 와 satisfied가 합쳐진 느낌이다. 뜻은 비슷하다. 혼자 뿌듯한 감정을 느끼는 것.

Content: 무엇이어도 나는 괜찮은 상태를 나타낼 때 쓰인다.

예문

I feel **content** on taking on more tasks than my colleagues for this project.
내가 다른 동료들보다 해야 할 일이 많지만 나쁘지 않아.
I feel **content** about our lesson.
학생: 이 수업 나쁘지 않아. (교수님이 들었을 때는 '불만족하는구나'라고 느낄 수 있음)

* 비슷한 단어: fine, okay, alright
  차이점 : content 무언가를 해야 하는 것에 거부감이 없을 때
  100% 행복한 게 아닌 60-65% 만족하고 행복한 느낌이다.

❋ 경력과 관련된 자격증 따기
I enjoy obtaining certifications that are related to my job

I enjoy obtaining certifications that are related to my job.
저는 제 일과 관련된 자격증들을 따는 것을 즐기는 편이에요.
I feel content by passing exams for certifications.
I feel content when I pass exams for certifications.
저는 자격증 시험을 통과함으로써 만족감을 느낍니다.

Obtain은 주로 격식(formal)있는 말로 '얻다(get)'에 형식적으로 많이 쓴다.
누군가에게서부터 직접적으로 얻었을 경우에는 쓰지 못한다.
Obtain은 누군가 나에게 직접 전달한 게 아니어도 되지만 receive는 누군가에게 직접적으로 전달받았을 때 쓰인다.

> **예문**

문서나 자격증을 받을 때 많이 쓰인다.
I need to obtain a certificate from city hall. (o)
I need to receive a certificate from city hall. (x)
시험을 통과하지 못한 상태에서 '나는 이것을 따야 해'라는 말을 하는 것은 부적합(receive는 내가 받을 자격이 있을 때 써야 한다. 얻어내는 것을 써야 할 때는 obtain이 적합하다.)하다.
I need to receive money from my friend. – 한 사람과 사람 사이에 받는 것이니 (O)
I need to obtain some documents from the city hall. – 직접적으로 받는 것이 아닌 한 큰 단체에서 누군가에게 받는 것이니 (O)
I want to receive a gift from Santa. (O) – Santa는 사람 (직접적인 사람) 산타 할아버지한테 선물 받고 싶다.
I want to obtain a gift from Santa. (X) – 여기서는 선물을 빼앗겠다는 느낌이 강하다(강제성이 있음) 산타 할아버지가 선물을 받아 내야겠다. (산타가 내게 선물을 주는지에 대한 여부는 상관하지 않은 채)

> **다른 예문**

In order to go scuba diving, you must obtain a certificate.
스쿠버 다이빙을 하기 위해 너는 자격증을 얻어야 한다. (노력해서 얻는 느낌)
In order to go scuba diving, you must receive a certificate.
Receive를 쓰면 시험만 치면 바로 받는 느낌이다. 운전면허 받아야 돼, 운전면허 따야 해 같은 느낌이 난다.
In order to work as an English teacher, you must obtain a TEFL certificate.
모든 예문에 get이 obtain을 대체할 수 있다.

* 문법 포인트

Build는 '짓다'라는 뜻도 있지만 '무언가를 높이다, 강력하게, 더 낫게 만들다'라는 뜻 있는데 일상생활에서 build 라는 단어는 예시와 같은 곳에도 많이 쓰인다.

예문

He wants to **build up** his career.
그는 그의 경력을 쌓기를 원한다.
Scarlett needs to **build up** her self-esteem.
스칼렛은 그녀의 자존감을 높일 필요가 있어.
People make a lot of efforts to **build** a better life.
사람들은 더 나은 삶을 위해 많은 노력을 해.
It will **build up** your muscle.
이것은 너의 근육을 키울 거야.

Build를 쓸 때와 Build up의 차이

Build는 무언가를 완성해 나가는 느낌
Build up은 무언가를 했을 때 발전시키다의 의미와 가까움.
'build his career' = '무언가를 완성해 나간다'라는 느낌
'build up her self-esteem' = 무언가를 발전시킨다.
'build a building' vs 'build up my reputation'
(형태가 있는: 건물을 짓다) vs (형태가 없는: 명성을 쌓다)
Build는 행동이 끝나고 결과가 나오는 종착점이 있는 경우
Build up은 끝이 없는 종착점이 안 보이는 경우

예문

건물을 지을 때(종착점이 있음/ 결과물이 확실히 보일 때)
I'm building the bridges.
세계는 건물을 계속 짓고 있다.
People will keep on building the bridges.
keep on + verb + ing
앞으로 계속 ~을 할 것이다.
보이지 않는 결과물을 지을 때/ 결과물이 언제 끝날지 모를 때)
Scarlett always tries to build up good relationships with her coworkers.

스칼렛은 항상 동료들과 좋은 관계를 쌓으려 노력한다.
A number of people make a lot of efforts to build up better credit scores.
많은 사람들이 좋은 신용도를 받으려고 많은 노력을 한다.

❋ 운동하기
Work out: Exercise: Engage in physical activities

I like to work out.
전 운동하는 것을 좋아해요.
I enjoy exercising.
전 운동하는 것을 즐겨요.
I love engaging in physical activities.
저는 육체적인 활동을 하는 것을 좋아해요.

* 스칼렛의 문법 포인트

주로 I like to exercise 혹은 I love work out을 많이 쓰는데 engage라는 단어를 써서 약~간 나의 말솜씨를 뽐내 보고 싶을 때 쓸 수 있다.

I love engaging in physical activities.
나는 육체적인 활동들을 참여하는 것을 좋아해요.

* Engage in: ~에 참여하다

❋ 영어 배우기 Learning English

I'm interested in learning English.
저는 영어 배우는 것에 관심이 있어요.
I love studying English.
저는 영어 공부하는 것을 매우 좋아해요.
I enjoy learning languages.
저는 언어 배우는 것을 즐겨요.

❈ 독서하기 Reading books

I love reading books relating to self-help genre.
저는 자기계발서와 관련된 장르를 읽는 것을 좋아해요.
I tend to(like to) read psychology books.
저는 심리학 책을 읽는 편입니다.
I enjoy reading non-fiction books.
저는 비소설 책을 읽는 것을 즐겨요.
I'm into reading fiction books these days.
전 요즘 소설 책 읽는 것에 푹 빠졌어요.

* 스칼렛의 문법 포인트와 예문
1. tend to 동사 ~하는 경향이 있다.
2. be +into + 동명사 & 명사 ~에 푹 꽂혔다

I tend to be very hasty.
저는 성급한 편이에요.
I tend to be punctual.
저는 시간을 엄수하는 편이에요.
I tend to go to café when I'm free.
저는 시간이 여유로울 때 카페에 가는 편이에요.
Scarlett tends to have dinner after work.
스칼렛은 퇴근 후 저녁을 먹는 편이에요.
Jen tends to be very detail-oriented while working.
젠은 일할 때 매우 섬세한 편이에요.

II

스칼렛
더 자세히
알아가기

1. 왜 그것들을 하세요?
Why do you like doing those activities? 중급/중상급

※ 남자친구란... A boyfriend is...

남자친구란... 참 복잡한 단어군.
어떤 때는 삶의 달콤한 에너지를 주는 사랑하는 한 사람이 될 수도 있는데 어떤 때는 나에게 독이 되는 사람이 될 수도 있을 것 같아.
잘 맞는 사람과 좋은 관계를 지내면 삶에서 아주 중요한 역할을 하는 사람이겠지만 그게 아니라면 시간을 낭비한 것 같은 안타까움을 주기도 하지.
사실 헤어진 지 얼마 안 돼서 철학적인 생각이 많은가 봐. 연애 상담이 필요하면 언제든지 알려줘!

Well, a boyfriend. It is a complicated word.
There are times a boyfriend can be a loved one who gives me positive vibes, however, there are times a boyfriend can be a negative influence providing me with toxic energy. I think if I have a good relationship with the right person, they can play a very important role in my life. Otherwise, it would be a pity to have wasted my time with that person.
Actually, I think I have a lot of philosophical thoughts because I recently just ended a romantic relationship. If you need any dating advice, let me know anytime.

* 스칼렛의 문법 포인트와 예문
1. complicating word가 아니라 complicated word인 이유
어떠한 단어를 의인화를 시킨 것: 편의를 위해 의인화를 시킨 것이다.
의인화 시키다: 사람이 아닌 것을 사람에 빗대어 표현하는 것을 말한다.
The boyfriend is a complicated word.
The boyfriend is a complicated person.

(word라는 단어가 person을 대체한 경우이다.)

2. 보통 ed가 들어가면 사람이 감정을 느끼고, ~인 상태로 쓰인다.
I'm interested, excited, confused... 등
반면에 ing가 들어가면 사물, 상황의 느낌을 표현할 때 쓰인다. → It is interesting, exciting, confusing....
감정 표현을 하는 단어에 ed가 붙는 것은 사람의 감정을 묘사 할 때 → He is excited to be at the concert. 그는 그 콘서트장에 있는 것이 신이 난다. (사람이 감정을 느끼고 있음)
I'm interested in learning vocabulary words.
나는 단어를 배우는 것에 흥미가 있어요.

3. 모두 주어가 사람이 느낌을 받고 있으면 동사 단어에 ed 붙이기
Interest, excite, confuse... 동사에 ing가 들어가면 상황의 상태를 이야기할 때 쓰인다.
This concert is very exciting.
이 콘서트는 정말 신이 나. (이 콘서트가 신이 나는 감정을 내뿜는다.)
This question is so confusing.
이 질문은 정말 헷갈려.(질문이 헷갈리는 감정을 내뿜는다)
This movie is so interesting.
이 영화는 정말 흥미로워.

---

* there are times 주어 + 동사 - ~할 때가 있다.
  There are times I want to watch sad movies. (슬픈 영화가 볼 때가 있어.)
  There were times I was very immature. (내가 매우 성숙하지 못할 때가 있었지.)
* positive vibes – (긍정적인 느낌), 좋은 느낌
* negative influence – 부정적인 영향
* provide – 제공하다, 주다
* toxic energy – 암 같은 존재, 부정적인 에너지
* right person – (나에게) 맞는 사람
* have a good relationship with ~와 좋은 관계를 가지다.

Play a /an 형용사 role in 명사 ~에서 (형용사)한 역할을 하다.

예

뚜렷한 계획들은 영어를 배우는 데 있어 중요한 역할을 한다.
- Clear goals play an important role in learning English.

  식이 조절은 건강해지기 위해 중대한 역할을 한다.
- Diet plays a crucial role in being healthy.

  프렌즈 어학원 선생님들은 스칼렛의 삶에서 중요한 역할을 했다.
- Friends academy teachers played an amazing role in Scarlett's life.

* because : 왜냐하면 사용법

  because 뒤에 주어 + 동사를 사용한다.

  because of 뒤에는 명사를 쓴다.

* otherwise – 그렇지 않으면[않았다면]
* pity – 동정(심), 불쌍히[측은히] 여김, 유감, 불쌍히 여기다
* philosophical - 철학에 관련된, 철학적인
* thoughts – 생각
* recently – 최근에
* end a relationship – 관계를 접다, 끝내다
* dating advice – 연애 팁
* let somebody know – 누군가에게 알리다
* anytime - 언제든지

* 같은 내용의 다른 문장

What is a boyfriend? I think the word itself is complicated.
It's a connection that can take your feelings on a roller coaster of emotions.
One minute, a boyfriend is someone who you love and cherish, who gives you nothing but warmth and sweet energy. And then another minute later, after a thoughtless comment, or a momentary miscommunication, or maybe it's been their personality all along, hidden behind sweetness—they can become the most negative person you've ever known. Filling you up with toxic energy. The definition of the word makes me think.
With the right person, at the right time, in the right way—they can

be the perfect person and play an important role in my life.
Otherwise, they'll strap me to a roller coaster train for a ride, and maybe never let me off.
I would waste my life on someone who doesn't care.
It would be a pity to waste my time on someone who didn't love me back.
Maybe I have these thoughts because I recently broke it off with someone whom I thought I loved. If you're having trouble too, let me know. Maybe we can talk about it, and I can help you out. I've always been great at listening.

* One minute = there are times = 언제는, 그때는
  예 One minute I am having a good day and the next, I spill my coffee and feel as though my entire day is ruined.

즐거운 하루를 보내고 있는 순간, 커피를 쏟고 나면 하루가 다 망가지는 기분이에요.

* connection - 연관성
* emotion - 감정
* cherish - 소중히 여기다, 아끼다
* warmth and sweet energy - 따뜻함과 포근함
* thoughtless comment- 무심한 /comment – 답변, 언급
* thoughtless reaction – 영혼 없는 반응
* momentary - 순간적인, 잠깐의
* miscommunication - 의사소통의 오류, 오해
* personality – 성격
* all along- 내내
* sweetness - 다정함, 상냥함
* fill someone up with – 어떤 사람을 무엇으로 채워주다
* definition - 정의
* right person – _____ (위에서 답 찾아보기)

> 예문

The right one will come around eventually.
결국에는 나랑 _____ 사람을 만날 거다.
* strap- 끈, 끈으로 묶다.
* break something off – (틀에서) 무언가를 벗어나다, 무언가를 깨고 나오다
* be 형용사 at + 동명사 = (동명사) 하는 것을 (형용사) 하다
> 예 I'm good at cooking = 전 요리 잘 해요.

❋ 술이란... Drinking is...

스트레스 풀기는 참 중요한 것 같아. 안 그러면 번아웃이 올 수도 있거든. 그래 본 적도 있고.
보통 몸에 좋지는 않지만 너무 스트레스를 받을 때면 자기 전에 맥주 한두 캔 정도 마시는 편이야. 술을 별로 좋아하지 않았었는데 술 맛에 빠져 버렸지 뭐야.
끊고 싶지만 끊고 싶지 않아. 뭔지 알지?
친구들이랑 마시면 그대로의 맛이 있고 혼자 마시면 혼자만의 재미가 있는 것 같아. 건강에 좋지는 않아서 끊어야지, 자주 생각은 하는데 인생 뭐 있니?

I think relieving stress is very important. Otherwise, you might get burned out.
I've been there before.
Drinking is usually not good for health, but when I'm stressed out, I drink a beer or two before I go to bed. I didn't like alcohol that much, but I fell in love with it.
I want to quit, but I don't want to stop. You know what I mean, right? If you drink with your friends, it can be such a joyful activity, and if you drink alone in moderation, it's also enjoyable. Drinking is not the healthiest activity, so I often think that I need to quit it but…. There's not too much to life.

---

* relieve – (스트레스 등을) 완화하다, 덜어주다
* get burned out – 번아웃 되다
* be stressed out – 스트레스를 받다
* fall in love with - ~와 사랑에 빠지다
* quit – (하던 것을) 그만두다
* I have been there – '그곳에 가 봤다'라고 해석할 수 도 있지만, '나도 그래 봤다'라고도 할 수 있다.
    예) I messed up on my mid-term.
    나 중간고사 망쳤어.
    I have been there; my mom was so upset about it.
    나도 (망쳐 봤어) 그래 봤지. (그래서) 우리 어머니께서 정말 화가 나셨었어.

> * such - 그런, 완전 강조하고 싶을 때
> * joyful – 아주 기뻐하는, 기쁨을 주는
> * in moderation - 적당히, 알맞게
> * enjoyable - 즐길 수 있는
> * I often think that I need to quit drinking - 나는 자주 내가 술을 끊어야 한다고 생각해.
> * I frequently (빈번히) go hiking. (나는 자주 등산을 간다.)
> * She rarely cooks at home. (그녀는 집에서 (요리를) 밥 잘 안 해 먹어.)
> * They sometimes meet together. (그들은 가끔 만난다.)
> * There's not too much to life. (인생 별거 없어)

Often ← 빈도 부사는 주어와 동사 사이 또는 Be 동사가 나올 경우 be동사 뒤에 나온다.

* 같은 내용의 다른 문장
You might form a different view of me when you hear this, but I think one of the ways I relieve my stress is through moderate amount of drinking.
It's not a positive habit. It isn't usually good for one's health either, but when I'm stressed out, I drink a beer or two before I go to bed.
I sometimes indulge myself in drinking to be in a relaxing mood whenever I'm writing a book or any other work that I need to get done.
At first, I didn't like alcohol that much, but after a while, I fell in love with it.
I fell in love with what it now does for me.
I want to quit, but I don't want to stop.
It's like a bad relationship that has me on the losing side. You know what I mean, right?
If you drink with your friends, it isn't so bad. Drinking with those you are close to
heightens the experience. Or drinking alone, when you are in an

enjoyable mood, a little way to celebrate the end of the day, isn't so bad either. It's when you're alone and at your lowest
I know it isn't healthy. So, I try not to drink when I feel down or depressed.

> * Heightens experience (순간) - 순간을 더욱 더 고조 시킨다. (평소보다 더 재미있고 부각시키는 순간)
> * It's when you are alone and at your lowest. - 특히 네가 (외롭고, 힘들 때) 그때 이래.
> * what it now does for me – (술이= what it) 현재 나에게 도움을 주는 것
> * Indulge – 사치 부리다
>   **예문** I'm going to indulge myself in a movie. I don't care about my failed exam. (영화나 봐야겠다. 시험도 망치고 에라 모르겠다.)
> * Be in a relaxing mood - 평온한 상태에서

❋ 친구랑 수다를 떠는 건... Chatting with friends is...

다들 요즘 너무 바빠서 만나는 것은 물론이고 전화하는 것도 쉽지 않지만 나는 항상 내 전화를 받아주는 친구들이 있어서 주로 스트레스를 받을 때 그 친구한테 전화해서 모든 걸 다 털어놓는 편이야.
왠지 모르게 화났던 모든 것을 털어놓고 나면 속이 많이 편해지는 것 같아.
말을 다 하고 나서는 가끔 후회하고 친구가 힘들까 봐 미안하기도 하지만 내 성격인 걸 어떡해? 그리고 너무 마음에 담아 놓는 것도 심적으로 좋지 않은 것 같아. 친구야, 미안해.

The world is evolving at such a crazy speed nowadays that I can't even meet and talk to my friends properly.
Luckily though, I do have some friends who do pick up my calls whenever I call them and we talk about everything.
A little bit of venting, can go a long way.
Sometimes I regret the things I say and I also feel sorry for my friends who have to deal with me constantly.

I can't help it. It's just what I do.
Why not let it all out? It's good for your psyche.
I do feel guilty about my sins sometimes.

> * evolving at(such a crazy speed) – 흘러가다(미친 듯이 빠르게)
> * nowadays - 요즘에는
> * properly - 제대로, 적절히
> * luckily though - 다행히도(운 좋게도)
> * pick up one's call – 내 연락을 받아주다
> * vent – (감정, 분통 등을) 터뜨리다
> * go a long way - 오래가다, 오래 지속되다
> * deal with - ~을 다루다
> * constantly – 끊임없이
> * can't help (but) - 어쩔 수 없다
> * express - 표현하다
> * psyche – 정신 건강
> * sins - 죄
> * Why not let it all out? - 다 풀어내는 게 어때?

* 문법 포인트

1. These days vs Nowadays ←차이점
크게 다르진 않지만 interchangeable = 교체 가능한
Nowadays = (adverb) 부사로 쓰임
These days = (noun) 명사로 쓰임

2. Nowadays have been boring (불가능)
* Nowadays: 최근에, 기간, 불투명한 시간, 부사('최근에' 형용사로 쓰였다 명사로 쓰인 게 아니어서 부적합하다.)
These days have been boring (가능)
* These days: 정확한, 구체적인 시간, 명사(These days가 구체적인 시간으로 명사로 쓰였다.)
These days & Nowadays 내용에 따라 달라질 수 있지만 These days는 내가 개인적(personal)으로 한 것을 이야기할 때 많이 쓰인다.

These days, I've been learning how to cook.
요즘 나는 요리하는 것을 배우고 있는 중이야.
These days, I've been studying English.
요즘 나는 영어 공부를 하는 중이야.

Nowadays 다른 사람에 대해 이야기할 때 많이 쓰인다.

People have hectic life styles nowadays.
사람들은 요즘에 매우 바쁜 삶에 스타일을 가지고 있다.
Scarlett is acting kind of funny nowadays.
스칼렛은 요즘에 좀 이상하게 행동하고 있어.

*** 같은 내용의 다른 문장**
Our lives are now more hectic than ever. Caught up in a fast-paced world, we rarely have time to meet with friends or call them on their phone these days.
I'm fortunate, though. I have some friends who always answer my calls no matter how busy they are with their own lives. Naturally, because I know they are there for me, I turn to them whenever I am stressed and tell them everything that I have on my mind.
For some reasons, they always make me feel better, and I can't imagine being unable to vent to my friends to lift my frustrations.
Sometimes, I regret everything I told them after hanging up the phone. I just couldn't stop the words from pouring out. I realize that I probably added to their own stress.
But I realize that this is part of my nature. I have the desire to express myself and cannot change who I am.
I am lucky for the friends I have, and I hope they know that I am here for them too. Knowing that they can complain to me, and ask me what to do when they have no one else to turn to.
I don't think it's good for our mental health to keep all our feelings to ourselves.

We need to let out our thoughts, feelings, and emotions from time to time.
I feel somehow sorry for my friend.

> * live의 복수 lives(3인칭 단수 동사에 s 붙인 게 아닌 것에 주의하자)
> * hectic - 정신없이 바쁜
> * caught up – catch up 따라가다, 소식 같은 것을, 소식을 접하다
> * fast-paced - 빠른 속도로
> * fortunate - 운 좋은, 다행인
> * naturally - 자연스럽게
> * unable - ~할 수 없는, ~하지 못하는
> * vent – _____ (위에서 답 찾아보기)
> * turn to = lean on - 기대다
> * for some reasons - 무슨 이유로, 어떤 까닭인지
> * we have to catch up. – 안부 나눠야지!
> 예 You have to catch up to the news. – 뉴스 좀 봐!
> * hang up the phone - 전화를 끊다
> * pour out – 쏟아져 나오다, (쌓아 두었던 감정, 말 등을) 쏟아 놓다
> * add - 더하다, 첨가하다
> * this is part of my nature. - 이게 내 본성의 중 (한) 부분이다.
> * desire – 바라다, 갈망하다
> * mental health - 정신 건강
> * let out our thoughts – 우리의 생각을 표출하다, 표출해라
> * from time to time – 가끔
> * somehow - 왠지, 왜 그런지(모르겠지만)

❋ 나의 경력 발전시키는 건... Building your career...

100세 시대가 된 이후로 나 자신을 계발시킬 필요는 있는 것 같다고 생각해. 뭔지 모르지만 다들 열심히 하니깐, 그리고 미래에 대한 불안함 때문에 항상 뭔가를 하긴 해야 할 것 같아. 21세기에 평생 직업은 없다고 하잖아.

꿈을 찾는 삶의 영어

Experts state that we will live past the age of 100. To be prepared for such a long life in a constantly changing world, I need to develop myself.
I don't know how, but everyone is working hard, and because of the feeling of anxiety, I need to be on the alert for my future.
In the 21st century, people say there is no such thing as a job that we can keep forever. Technology, artificial intelligence, and globalization will completely alter the future of labor.

* expert - 전문가
* state - (정식으로) 말하다[쓰다], 진술하다
* live past the age of 100 - 100세 이상을 살다
* long life – 장수
* constantly – _____ (위에서 답 찾아보기)
* work hard – 열심히 일하다
* anxiety - 불안, 염려
* I don't know how, but – 뭔지 모르지만, …
* be on alert – 경계 태세를 갖추다. (항상 정신 차리고 있다)
  예 be on your alert – 군대에서 "경계 태세를 늦추지 마" 이럴 때도 쓰인다.
* keep forever – 영원히 가지다
* technology - 기술
* artificial intelligence - 인공지능
* completely - 완전히, 전적으로
* future of labor – 근로 환경의 미래

* **같은 내용의 다른 문장**

Experts tell us that, in the future, we will live past the age of 100. This number used to be much lower, but now as the technology advances, we expect to see changes, one being longevity. But this also means that our lifestyles must change.
It is a challenge to keep up with this constantly changing world. I realize that in order to keep up with everyone else, I need to make plans of my own. I need to develop into someone who can adapt to

these changes as they come, instead of struggling in a race where I am losing against all the other competitors. Somehow, people around me are working very hard. They're more diligent than I am. Seeing them like this gives me a sense of anxiety. But I try to use these negative feelings in a positive way. I use this nervousness to get me moving forward like everyone else. It gets me thinking about how I can be prepared for my future.

In the 21stcentury,peoplesaythatitisimpossibletofindajobwewillkeep forever.

Technology, artificial intelligence, and globalization will completely alter the future of labor.

Therefore, as our world changes, so must we. As jobs change, so must our skills. Or else, we must fear a new assailant of being left behind.

* expert – _____ (위에서 답 찾아보기)
* advance - (지식 기술 등이) 증진되다[진전을 보다]
* longevity – 장수, 오래 지속되는 무엇
* keep up – 뒤떨어지지 않게 나 자신도 같이 따라가다
* adapt to - ~에 적응하다
* struggle – 투쟁하다, 몸부림치다, 버둥거리다
* competitor - 경쟁자
* somehow – _____ (위에서 답 찾아보기)
* diligent - 부지런한
* nervousness - 긴장감
* get someone moving forward – 누구를 앞으로 가게 한다
* so must we – (Old English grammar): we must do the same (Modern grammar) - 우리도 그렇게 해야 한다
* so must our skills (Old English grammar) - (Our skills must be updated) – 우리도 현대 흐름에 따라가야 한다, 우리도 가진 기술을 발전시켜야 한다.

※ 경력과 관련된 자격증 따기
Obtaining certifications relating to my job

취업 시장은 점점 경쟁이 치열해지고 있어. 나 자신을 계발시키는 방법 중 하나는 자격증을 따는 것 같아. 물론 실력도 쌓을 수 있지만 자존감을 높이기 위한 방법 중 하나랄까?
난 요즘 토익이랑 오픽 공부를 하고 있어. 이건 필수라고 하니깐 뒤처질 필요는 없잖아?

Since the job market has been getting more competitive, I think one of the ways to develop myself is more and more clearly getting a certification. Of course, you can build up your skills, but getting a certification is one of the efficient ways to boost your self-esteem. These days, I've been studying for TOEIC and OPIC exams. People think that it is an essential certificate to acquire and I don't want to be left behind, right?

* competitive - 경쟁력 있는, 경쟁이 심한
* develop - 개발하다, 성장하다
* build up - 쌓아 올리다, 증진시키다
* certification - 자격증, 증명
* efficient - 능률적인, 효율적인

매우 유용한 단어 boost! - 신장시키다, 북돋우다

Energy drinks boost your energy.
에너지 드링크는 당신의 에너지를 북돋습니다.
It will help you boost your credit score.
이것은 당신의 신용도를 올리는 데 도움이 될 것입니다.
Self-help books sometimes help you boost your confidence.
자기계발서는 가끔씩 당신이 자신감을 북돋우는 데 도움이 됩니다.
* self-esteem - 자존감
* be left behind - 뒤에 남게 되다

* 같은 내용의 다른 문장

The world is a competitive place. Over the years, securing a good job has been a challenge. Since the job market has been getting more difficult, it has become harder to even find a decent job to apply for. We need to bolster our chances by using every possible method to advance up the ladder.

After reflecting on my observations, I have begun to consider what will set me apart from all other applicants. I think one of the ways to develop myself seems to be getting a certification or several depending on what skills a hiring company might seek.

The job market demands highly skilled candidates.

Of course, you can build up your skills without certifications through getting experience and establishing your resume. However, certifications tend to have an added benefit. They tend to help you feel the boost in your self-esteem.

These days, I've been studying for TOEIC and OPIC tests. People consider these to be essential certifications to have, and I don't want to be left behind. As long as we keep on top of progressing towards the next step, we will never be left behind!

---

* competitive – _____ (위에서 답 찾아보기)
* secure something – 무언가를 확보하다
* bolster – 촉진하다, 발전시키다, 강화하다
* advance up: moving up the ladder – 단계를 밟아 나아가다
* reflect on - ~을 되돌아보다
* observation - 관찰, 감시, 주시
* demand - 필요로 하다, 요구되다
* candidate – 후보자, 입후보자
* benefit - 혜택, 이득
* essential - 필수적인, 극히 중요한
* applicant - 지원자
* ladder - (사회 속) 계급, 단계
* set a part from - ~에서부터 동떨어진

❈ 영화 보는 건... Watching movies is...

영화 보는 것은 참 재미있는데, 혼자 집에서 영화를 보는 건 영화가 정말 재미있지 않으면 집중하는 게 쉽지 않은 것 같아. 그래서 가끔 나는 혼자 영화가 보고 싶으면 영화관에 가서 보는 편이야.
남자친구가 있을 때는 많은 영화를 집에서 자주 봤던 것 같아.
누군가랑 같이 볼 때는 참 재미있어. 내가 가장 좋아하는 영화를 말해보자면 〈패치아담스〉랑 〈인턴〉이라는 영화야. 나는 사실 같은 영화를 다시 보는 걸 좋아하지는 않는데 저 영화들은 계속 봐도 질리지가 않아.

Watching movies is great, but I find it hard to concentrate if the movie itself isn't enjoyable.
So, when I want to watch a movie alone, I go to the movie theater.
I think I watched a lot of movies at home when I had a boyfriend.
It's a lot more fun to watch with someone. When it comes to fun movies, Patch Adams and The Intern are some of my favorites. I generally don't really like to re-watch movies, but I never get sick of these movies.

---

* concentrate - 집중하다
* enjoyable - 즐거운
* when it comes to: ~와 관련하여
  - 예 (영어에 관련한 거라면 그 선생님이 가장 잘 가르치지!)
    When it comes to English, that teacher is the best!
    (스칼렛은 오픽에 대해서 모든 것을 아는 것처럼 아는 척을 했어.)
    Scarlett pretended to know that she knows everything when it comes to OPIC.
* re-watch - (명사, 동사 가능) – 다시 보다, 재방송(하이프네이션: 보통 명사격으로 쓰인다)
  - 예 The Friends is a good re-watch. (프렌즈는 재방송으로 보기 좋은 프로그램이다.)
    Scarlett always re-watches the movie on weekends. (스칼렛 주말마다 항상 그 영화를 다시 본다.)

> * be / get + sick (and tired) + of +동명사 – (동명사에) 싫증이 나다, 질리다
>   예 I'm sick and tired of : 진절머리가 나다
>   I'm sick and tired of doing house chores! (집안일 하는 데 진절머리가 나!)
>   He is getting tired of studying the subject. (그는 그 과목을 공부를 하는 것이 너무 질려요.) (약간 약하게 말할 때)
>   They got sick of drinking by now. (그들은 술 마시는 게 이제는 질려요.)
> * concentrate (on) 집중하다: focus on과 거의 비슷하지만 Concentrate on – 무언가를 하나만 집중하는 것(지금 현재 한 분야에만 집중)
>   예 Can you leave me alone? I need to concentrate on my exam. (나 좀 혼자 놔둘래? 나 시험공부해야 해.)
>   Focus on – 평소의 나의 모든 집중을 무언가에 전체적으로 쏟고 있는 것 I'm currently focusing on my career. –지금 현재 나는 나의 커리어(경력)에 집중하고 있다.

* 같은 내용의 다른 문장

Watching movies is a great activity, but if the movie isn't captivating, I find it difficult to watch. I think back to when I used to watch movies at home, and that makes me miss watching with someone. I also miss seeing their expressions change as they watch the same screen as me. Hearing them laugh as I laugh or gasp at the same time at something frightening, even shedding tears when the hero dies. I wasn't alone in my feelings.

Maybe that's why my favorite movies are Patch Adams and The Intern. I want to watch something heart-warming or funny to chase away the absence at my side.

While I generally dislike re-watching movies, I never seem to tire of these two.

> * activity - 활동
> * captivating - 마음을 사로잡는
> * give someone (the/an) impression - 누구에게 인상을 주다
> * gasp - 숨이 턱 막히다, 허업 하고 숨을 쉬다

* at the same time – 동시에
* frightening - 무서운
* shedding tears – 눈물을 흘리다
* heart-warming - 마음이 따뜻해지는
* chase away - ~을 쫓아내다
* absence at my side - 나에게 비어 있는 무언가(공허함)

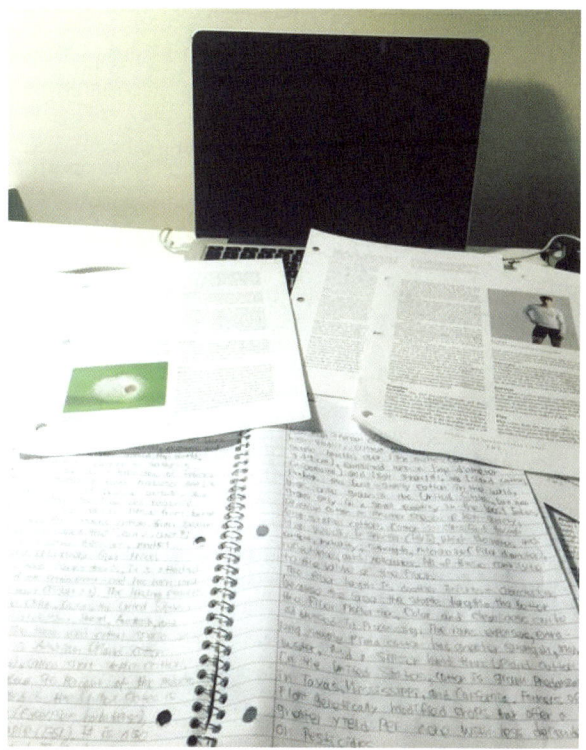

❊ 공부란... Studying is important because...

인생에서 많은 기회를 주는 공부는 내가 좋아하는 것을 찾기 시작하게 되면 날개 같은 존재가 될 수도, 의미 없이 하는 공부는 지옥과 같은 느낌을 주는 존재가 될 수 있다고 생각해.
공부는 언제 하든 늦은 때란 없는 것 같아.
공부는 학생 때부터 성인이 되어서도 끝없이 해야 하는 과목이지.
자격증도 따고 회사 공부도 해야 되고, 바쁘다 바빠!

In my opinion, studying which provides us of a number of opportunities, can give you a head- start. However, if we do it meaninglessly it can be like hell.
I believe in the saying "It is never too late to pick up on studying."
Studying is a subject that we should study endlessly.
I need to study for certifications and work; I don't even have the time to breathe!

---

* provide – _____ (위에서 답 찾아보기)
* a number of – 다수의, 얼마간의
* opportunities – 기회
* It is never too late to pick up on studying – 공부는 언제 시작해도 늦은 게 아니다.
* Better late than never – 아예 안 하는 것보다 늦게 하는 게 낫다= 늦은 때란 없다)
* It's never too late to 동사 – (동사)하기에 늦은 때란 없다
* head-start – (남보다 일찍 시작해서 갖게 되는) 유리함
* meaninglessly - 무의미하게
* believe in - ~을 믿다
* endlessly - 끊임없이, 무한히
* breathe - 호흡하다, 숨을 쉬다

* 같은 내용의 다른 문장

Studying gives us a number of opportunities. Both now and for our futures.

These opportunities are a pair of wings we grow ourselves through hard work and dedication.

if we do not condition our wings, however, they will wither and bring us down—like a bird shot out of the sky. Studying can be like hell sometimes. I won't deny this. It can make you feel like you are falling.

Yet, I do not ever think it is too late in your life to try to fly and soar into the sky higher than you ever were before.

Studying is something we should pursue endlessly.

We need to become better version of ourselves and be curious about the world!

However, take it slow if you need to. Get your wings to grow before attempting to fly. Make them strong, and then take off!

> * dedication - 헌신
> * if we do not condition our wings – 우리의 날개(능력) 관리하지 않으면
> * condition – 관리하다, 길들이다
> * a bird shot out of the sky – 총을 맞아 땅으로 떨어지는 새처럼
> * deny - 부인하다, 인정하지 않다
> * wither - 메말라 죽다
> * soar into - 치솟다
> * pursue - 추구하다
> * become better version of - 더 나은 내가 되기 위해서
> * attempt - 시도하다
> * take off – 이륙하다, 날아오르다

2. 자기계발이란...
Self-improvement is...

❋ **일찍 일어나기 Getting up early.**

미라클 모닝이라고 들어봤어? 아루나루는 한국어로 아침, 저녁 루틴의 줄임말이야. 아침 일찍 일어나서 하루를 더 효율적으로 보내는 거야.

요즘에는 소셜미디어로 이것저것 많이 하잖아. 그중에 '아루나루'라고 카카오톡 그룹 채팅으로 50 - 80명의 사람들이 매일매일 일어난 사진을 인증하면서, 일찍 일어나서 한 다양한 일들을 인증하는 모임도 있어!

Have you heard of Miracle Morning?
Arunaru is a short for morning routine and evening routine in Korean. Also, it means getting up early in the morning and spending the day more efficiently.
These days, people do a lot of things on social media.
Among them, there is a group chat called 'Arunaru' where 50-80 people are in the group and they share the pictures after getting up or things that they decided to do in the group chat.
They share various activities that they have done in the group chat!

> * short for – 무엇의 줄임말
> * shorten - 단축하다

* 문법 포인트

be동사 + p.p.(과거분사) -되어지다 수동태!

> * arunaru is shortened for - 아루나루는 단축된 단어야.
> * routine - 일상
> * get up - 일어나다
>   get up과 wake up의 차이점: get up은 신체적으로 일어나는 것이고 wake up은 눈이 떠진, 정신적으로 깬 상태를 나타낸다.
> * efficiently - 효과적으로
> * social media: SNS 우리가 말하는 SNS를 말하기보단 Social media로 쓰인다. = SNS라고 하면 원어민들은 이해할 수 없다.
> * among – 몇몇 사이에 between은 (둘) 사이에, among은 (3개 이상 사이)를 말할 때 쓴다.
> * share - 나누다

* 문법 포인트

After /before 뒤에는 동명사나 주어 동사가 와야 한다.

🔵 예 After I read Scarlett's book I was so touched.
 (스칼렛의 책을 읽고 나는 감동받았다.)
 Before reading Scarlett's book, I was already touched.
 (스칼렛의 책을 읽기 전에 이미 감동을 받았다.)

🔵 예
After I read Scarlett's book I was so touched.

> * various - 다양한
> * activities – 활동들

* 같은 내용의 다른 문장

Have you ever heard of a Miracle Morning?
How we begin our days will determine how they end.
Arunaru is a term for a daily routine in Korea. Arunaru means getting up early and being productive right from the start. The most important parts of our day are how we begin and how we end.

Everything else in between is a response to how we enter our day. No sleeping in or hitting the snooze button, otherwise the day will start without you.

These days, people seem to do everything on social media. While not all of it is positive, there are groups that help motivate one another towards a healthier life style. Among these numerous groups, there is one chat called "Arunaru" where 50-80 people share their pictures after getting up or the things that they have accomplished at the start of their day in the group chat. By posting what they have done, even if it is just getting out of bed on time, these members help to motivate those with difficult mornings.

Sometimes all it takes is the reminder of a great day waiting for us, so long as we can get up and go!

* determine - (공식적으로) 확정[결정]하다
* is a term for – 이 (단어)는 ~을 위한 용어이다
* be a response to - 어떤 것에 대한 답변이 되다
* sleep in – 늦잠 자다
* so long as – 이렇게만 하면
* otherwise – _____ (위에서 답 찾아보기)
* motivate - 동기를 부여하다
* numerous: several - 수많은
* accomplished - 성취한 게 많은
* at the start of – (무엇의) 시작점에서
* post - 게시하다
* reminder - 상기시키는(생각나게 하는) 것

❋ 운동하기... Exercising is...

하, 마음속으로는 진짜 매일 운동하는데.... 하루는 열정이 타올랐다가도 이틀 정도 지나면 왜 이렇게 게을러지는지 모르겠어. 나는 그래도 주 2-3회 정도는 운동을 하려고 노력을 해. 성공하는 사람들 대부분 운동을 하잖아.
나는 체력 때문에 운동을 하려 하는데 평생의 싸움이 되지 않을까 싶어. 다행히도 운동을 안 하면 몸이 많이 무거워서 안 가는 날엔 오히려 더 힘들어지고 있어. 운동을 하는 날에는 상쾌하면서도 뿌듯할 때가 많은 것 같아.

In my heart, I work out every day, but I don't know why I get so lazy after a day or two. I still try to exercise two to three times a week. You know, most successful people work out on a consistent basis. I'm trying to exercise to improve my energy level, but I think it'll be a lifelong struggle.

But thankfully, if I don't exercise, I know that my body would get chubbier, so if I don't go to the gym, I feel more tired. When I do go to the gym and work out, I feel a sense of pride and feel refreshed. Exercise is a great remedy for reducing my level of stress and increasing my level of happiness.

---

* In my heart – 내 마음속
* on my mind – (현재 내가 가지고 있는) 생각

  The upcoming exam is always on my mind. (다가올 시험이 항상 머리에 맴돌고 있다.)
  The regret of not having gone to a four year university has always been on my mind. (4년제 대학을 안 간 후회가 아직까지도 내 머리 속에 맴돌고 있다.)
  I keep you in my heart. (난 너를 마음에 항상 담고 있어.)
  Hailey, whom I've met in Canada while I was studying there, will always be in my heart. (내가 캐나다에서 공부할 때 만난 헤일리는 항상 내 마음속에 간직할 것이다.)

> * successful - 성공한, 출세한
> * on a consistent basis – 꾸준하게 하는
> * improve my energy level - 나의 체력을 향상시키다
> * lifelong – 평생 동안, 일생 동안
> * thankfully - 고맙게도, 다행스럽게도
> * chubbier - 더 통통한, 더 토실토실한
> * feel sense of pride - 자부심을 느끼다
> * refreshed – 상쾌한
> * remedy - 해결책, 개선책, 치료
> * reduce one's level of stress – 누군가의 스트레스 수치를 줄이다.
> * increase one's level of happiness - 누군가의 행복지수를 증가시키다.

* 같은 내용의 다른 문장

Even If I start out dedicated from the start, where my heart is set on the goal of working out every day, I can't seem to move past working out for a day or two in a row.

However, I don't let this bother me.

Even if it isn't what I set out to achieve at the beginning of the week, I still exercise two to three times a week. I try to look at things positively. An achievement is still an achievement in my book.

You know, most people who are successful work out on a consistent basis.

It's because of my energy. I am trying to exercise to improve how much energy I have.

But I think this will be a life-long battle between my body and I.

Yet, I am kind of thankful. Not going to the gym can be motivating in itself.

Not working out makes me feel heavier and less energized, and I hate this feeling.

Each time I make it to the gym and complete my workout, I feel energized and proud of my achievement.

Even if it's inconsistent, exercise is a great remedy for reducing my stress levels and increasing my overall level of happiness. When I am feeling down, then I know it's time to head off to the gym!

> * I set out to finish my project this week. (이번 주 내 프로젝트를 끝내려고 결심했다.)
> * an achievement is still an achievement.: 작은 성취도 나에게는 성취는 성취다
> * in my book = to me: 나에게는
> * battle - 싸우다, 투쟁하다
> * complete - 끝내다, 완료하다
> * inconsistent – 내용이 다른, 모순이 되는
> * head off to – 어디로 떠나다

* **문법 포인트**

1. start out + 형용사 = 어떤 상태로 ~을 하겠다

예문

start out dedicated - 헌신을 해서 ~을 하겠다
start out excited - 신난 상태에서 ~을 하겠다
I've started out dedicated at first, but I lost flame after a while. (처음에는 열심히 시작했다가 끝에 가서는 (열정이) 식어 버렸다.)
I will start out dedicated and I'm going to try to maintain the same level of dedication throughout. (처음에 열심히 시작해서 끝까지 유지하겠다.)

2. Every day vs Everyday 띄어쓰기 유무에 따른 차이점!
Everyday는 명사를 꾸며주는 형용사의 역할을 한다.

예문

Watching TV is an everyday occurrence for me. (TV를 보는 것은 나에게 매일 있는 일상이다.)

* occurrence – 발생하는 것

Reading is an everyday activity for me. (읽는 것은 나에게 매일 일어나는 활동이다.)
every day -매일 (빈도를 나타내는 부사)

예문

Scarlett drinks coffee every day. (스칼렛은 커피를 매일 마신다.)
Jay goes to the gym every day. (제이는 매일 헬스장에 간다.)

3. Work out vs exercise: 운동하다= 차이점은?
Exercise: 구체적인 운동을 할 때, 요가, 필라테스 등.
To work out: (명사로 쓸 때는 workout 붙여서 쓴다)
여러 개의 운동을 한 번에 할 때(단순 체력 단련으로 목적으로 여러 가지 운동: 특정 운동이 아님)

4. Successful? Success? Succeed?: 차이점
Successful(형용사): describing something that has been achieved: (어떤 일에) 성공한, 성공적인

예문

For me, a successful lesson is where students can feel satisfaction from them. (학생 만족도가 높아야 성공적인 수업이라고 생각합니다.)
Successful students tend to be hard-workers. (성공적인 학생은 부지런한 경향이 있습니다.)

Success (명사) : the accomplishment of an aim or purpose :성과, 성공

예문

I have had many successes in my life.
나는 내 삶에서 많은 성공을 해오고 있다.
I gained success when I put in a lot of efforts.
나는 노력을 많이 했을 때 성공을 누렸다.

Succeed – (<u>동사</u> 하려던 일에) 성공하다
To do what you are trying to do: to achieve the correct or desired result

예문

In order to succeed, you must put in a lot of efforts. (성공을 하기 위해서 너는 많은 애를 써야 한다.)
I will succeed because I am very motivated. (나는 매우 동기 부여가 됐으니 성공할 거야.)

사람의 소유격을 나타낼 때 (', 's)를 쓰지만 사물의 경우 (of)를 써 준다.

> 예문

Scarlett(사람)'s book is inspiring! (스칼렛'의' 책은 영감을 줘.)
I ate cake's(사물) piece. (x) 케이크는 사물이니 케이크 한 조각: 사물의 무엇이니 Of가 적합하다.
I ate a piece of cake(사물). (o) (소유격이 아님)

❋ 영어를 배우는 건... Studying English is...

한국에서 영어 공부는 필수인 것 같아. 요즘 중국어, 스페인어, 일본어 등등 많이 배우지만 영어는 기본적인 게 된 것 같아. 그리고 영어는 끝없는 공부가 되지 않을까 싶어.
영어를 잘하려면 영어에 미치거나 확실한 목표가 있어야 되는 것 같아.
이게 힘들면 절실하게 배워야 하는 상황을 만들어 보는 것도 도움이 되지 않을까? 해외에 뛰어든다거나, 영어를 배울 수 있는 직업을 한번 가져 본다든가.... 너무 뜬금없나?

I think studying English is kind of unavoidable in Korea. Although many people learn Chinese, Spanish and Japanese, I think English has become a language that we must learn.
And I feel like learning English is going to be an endless journey.
In order to be a fluent English speaker, we need to be into learning English or having a clear goal. If it seems to be too challenging, how about changing the scene that requires you to feel desperate about learning English or jumping abroad or having a job where English is essential? Do I sound too random?

> * unavoidable - 불가피한, 어쩔 수 없는
> * endless journey – 끝없는 여정
> * fluent - 유창한
> * kind of – 약간 (구어체로는= kinda) 약간의, 어느 정도(미국인이 많이 쓰는 자연스러운 표현으로 손바닥을 쫙 펴고 왼쪽 오른쪽으로 흔들며 많이 쓴다.)
>
> 예문
>
> "이게 바로 그런 거야?" "으, 응. 약간 그런?(손 왼쪽 오른쪽 흔들흔들)"
> * endless - 끝없는, 한없는
> * require - 요구하다, 필요로 하다
> * be + out of the blue – 뜬금없다.
>
> 예문
>
> It's out of the blue, did you know that? (뜬금없지만 너 그거 알았어?)
> * Random 무작위의, '닥치는 대로'도 비슷한 뜻으로 사용할 수 있다.
>
> 예문
>
> Can I ask a random question? (내가 뜬금없는 질문 좀 해도 될까?)

* 문법 포인트

1. In order to와 To

In order to: 무언가를 할 수 있게끔 하기 위해

예문

In order for me to become a good pianist, I have to practice a lot. (좋은 피아니스트가 되기 위해서는 연습을 많이 해야 한다.)
In order to는 목적(Purpose)이 있을 때 쓰인다. ~가 되기 위한, 하기 위한 '목적'
To: to부정사 동사 + to: 단순하게 하다, 매우 다방면으로 ~위해, 것 등으로 쓰인다. (동사와 목적어를 연결해 주는 의미)

2. 주어 + feel like + 동명사 - : 오늘 -가 땡긴다, - 하고 싶다.

예문

I feel like eating tteokbokki. (떡볶이가 땡긴다.)
He felt like hiking. (그는 등산이 가고 싶었어요.)

3. Aboard – 해외로 * overseas 와 abroad의 차이점은?
뉴앙스적인 차이
overseas는 '해외에서 (뭘 했다)'
abroad는 '해외로 (뭘 하러 갔다)'

예문

I studied overseas. (외국에서 공부했다.)
I went abroad to study overseas. (난 유학하려고 외국으로 갔다.)

* 같은 내용의 다른 문장

I think that studying English is an inevitable reality in Korea. I mean, it is a globally utilized language, after all. Although many people learn Chinese, Spanish, and Japanese, I think English has taken priority on what is most used around the world and where we should focus our attention. Yet, just like exercise, I feel that learning English will be an endless journey.

To be a fluent English speaker, you need to look at your approach.

If you aren't passionate, don't have faith in yourself, or don't have a goal, you will find the journey of English challenging. Start with baby steps. Look at yourself. What does English mean to you?

Is it for work, your social status, or maybe for personal growth?

Whatever the reason may be, if you see it as an obstacle in your future, it might be best to jump into it headlong and give yourself the sensation of desperation.

Apply for that studying abroad program! Get that job that forces you to use English! Get out there and get moving! Your future is bright, and it is waiting for you!

---

* Inevitable - 불가피한, 필연적인
* utilize - 활용하다
* take priority on – 어떤 것을 우선으로 삼아라
* attention - 주의, 주목, 관심
* approach - 접근하다, 접근법
* faith - 믿음

> * social status – 사회적 지위
> * obstacle – 장애, 장애물
> * jumping into something headlong = (뒤돌아보지 말고) 올인해라, 하나에 몰두하다.
> * desperation – 절실함
> * sensation - 느낌, 감각, 센세이션
> * start with baby steps = take baby steps – 처음부터 차근차근 시작하다
> * give yourself the sensation of desperation = 절심함이 무엇인지 느껴보세요.

❋ 독서하는 것은... Reading book is...

자기 계발 중에 하나를 꼽자면 당연히 독서라고 할 수 있겠지? 어떤 때는 책이 술술 읽히는데 어떤 때는 정말 안 읽히고 읽기 귀찮을 때가 많은 것 같아.
그래도 몰입해서 읽힐 때 자주 느끼는 건 정말 나는 우물 안 개구리였다는 걸 느끼기도 해.
그렇게 신세계를 느끼고 감탄을 하다가 또 어느 순간에는 책 읽는 흐름이 끊기기도 해서 아쉽기도 하지.
정리가 안 되고 뜬금없을 수 있지만 나도 책을 매일 읽는 멋진 사람이 되고 싶다.

Phew....
If I have to choose a self-development activity, reading books is going to be one of them. There are times when reading is a second nature to me, but there are other times it is difficult to read and it becomes a chore afterwards.
However, after immersing myself in reading, I felt as if I were a small fish in a big pond.
I was so impressed by reading and felt that I found a new world, but at a certain point, I felt sorry that the flow of my concentration was interfered.
I want to be a person who reads a book every day.

* there are times 주어 + 동사: ~ 할 때도 있다.

  예문

  There are times I feel lonely. (나도 가끔 외로울 때가 있지.)
  There are times I feel like watching horror movies. (가끔 무서운 영화 보고 싶을 때가 있어.)
* 과거로도 응용해 보기!
  There were times I had a hard time with burdens. (힘든 상황 때문에 어려운 때가 있었어.)
* a self-development activity – 자기계발 활동, 자기발달
* reading is a second nature to me - (책) 읽는 것은 나에게 너무 자연스러운 것이다.
* a second nature to me – 나한테는 너무 자연스러운 것이다.
* chore - (하기 싫은, 귀찮은) 일
* afterwards - 나중에, 그 뒤에
* immerse – ~에 몰두하다, 몰두하게 만들다
* As if + 가정법 과거 - 마치 ~인 것처럼
  As if I were 실제로 (간단히 생각하면) 실제가 아니라 가정하는 것이니 be 동사를 과거로!
* small fish in a big pond – 우물 안 개구리
* be impressed by - ~에 의해 감명을 받다
* at a certain point – 어느 시점에
* '아쉽다'라는 말을 한 단어로 설명하는 단어는 미국에 없다. 상황에 따라 I feel sad, frustrated, sorry, bad 등을 쓰면 그 감정을 담을 수 있다.
* flow - 흐름
* state - 상태
* concentration – 집중

* **같은 내용의 다른 문장**

Phew...

This is the one. If I have to choose an activity to throw on my growing list of self-improvements, reading is definitely one of them. There are times where I read books without issue, and then there

are other times that I just can't seem to force myself to keep going. This is when it becomes bothersome.
A book should be enjoyable, not a struggle.
However, after immersing myself successfully in a good book, I feel as though I am a small fish in a big pond. The book absorbs me like water and puts me in a brand-new world.
I hunger for this experience, and I feel a little guilty when I am unable to join in on the story. Sometimes, I just can't concentrate. I might have too much on my mind, or the story isn't what I need at that moment.
Yet, despite this struggle, I want to be the type of person that reads a book every day.

* this is the one – 바로 이거야
* throw on my growing list of self-improvements – 이미 긴 리스트에 무엇을 또 추가하다
* bothersome - 귀찮은 일, 성가신
* the book absorbs me like water. (책이 물처럼 나를 삼킨다.(흡수한다))
* brand-new – 아주 새로운
* hunger for – ~을 갈망하다
* feel a little guilty – 죄책감을 느끼다
* unable – ~할 수 없는
* I have too much on my mind. – 머릿속에 뭔가가 많다.
* at that moment – 그때에
* despite(something) – ~에도 불구하고

3. 스트레스를 주로 언제 받아요?
When do you usually get stressed?

❋ **직장/사회생활 Work & Social Life**

내가 스트레스를 받을 때라....
나는 내가 실수를 하면 온종일 그 생각을 하는 것 때문에 가끔 힘들곤 해.
또 내가 정해진 시간이 있는데, 한두 번도 아니고 그걸 더 요구하는 것을 당연히 여기면 너무 불공평하다고 생각해서 스트레스를 많이 받는 것 같아.
특히 무보수로 야근을 은근히 요구하는 직장에 있을 때 정말 스트레스를 많이 받았던 것 같아.
그리고 나는 집순이가 아니어서 집에만 하루 종일 있으면 왠지 모르게 스트레스를 받아. 뭔가를 하러 나가야 하는 편인 것 같아.

When I'm stressed out....
I tend to be obsessed with thinking about past mistakes and I think about them all day long. This gives me a hard time.
Additionally, when I have my own shift, if the boss asks me to work overtime every now and then, it's fine but if it consists, naturally I would think that it is UNFAIR.
It stresses me out and leaves me feeling bitter.
I think I was really stressed out especially when I had a job that required overtime without pay.
Since I'm not a homebody, I require a constant flow of some things to do. If I'm not getting that fixation, I tend to go out to do something kind of randomly.

* obsessed with (긍정, 부정일 때 둘 다 쓰일 수 있음)

My son is obsessed with Fortnite. (negative)

　　　　　　　* Fortnite –보통 아이들이 하는 배그 같은 게임

I'm obsessed with BTS nowadays. (neutrally positive) – 긍정, 부정 다 됨

I'm obsessed with watching Aran's Youtube Videos. – 나는 아란의 유튜브에 푹 빠졌어.

* pastmistakes – 과거의 실수들
* all day long – 온종일, 아침부터 밤까지
* additionally – 게다가
* shift – (교대 근무) 시간, 근무 시간
* unfair – 불공평한
* feel bitter – 씁쓸함을 느끼다
* require – 필요로 하다
* overtime – 야근, 잔업
* homebody – 집순이
* a constant flow of = 무언가를 지속적으로 하는 (flow= 흐름, 분위기, 상황)
* fixation = (나를 만족시켜 주는) 방법
* be stressed out: 스트레스를 받다
* tend to – _____ (위에서 답 찾아보기)

* 같은 내용의 다른 문장

This is a little difficult to confess, but we all must be a little guilty of it. When I'm stressed out....

I tend to obsess over revisiting my past mistakes. I think about them all day long.

What I could have done differently, what I should have done to change the trajectory of my life. What I would do differently if I could go back in time and change.

All these thoughts give me a hard time.

At the same time, I think it's natural.

When someone hires you for a specific shift, they shouldn't ask for more.
Working overtime once or twice is okay, but if your boss thinks that they can demand it out of you because you are willingly be taken advantage of due to your situation — they are just being abusive, right?
I think it's unfair that they tug us around like that.
Everyone needs work to get by.
I used to have a job where I worked overtime without pay.
Working overtime takes time away from me. I need time to breathe, time to live. And if I am always working, I never have time for either if I have the day off; I am out and about, looking for something new to try. But I also do this when I am stressed because I want to take my mind off of what is troubling me.

* confess – 자백하다, 인정하다
* obsess over revisiting my past mistakes – 과거의 내 실수들을 바꾸는 것에 집착하다.
* obsess – 집착하다
* revisit – 재방문하다, 되돌아보다
* trajectory – (인생의) 방향 (= orbit: 궤도)
* hire – 고용하다
* demand – _____ (위에서 답 찾아보기)
* willingly – 자진해서, 기꺼이
* I get bitter, too. - 나도 씁쓸해질 때가 있다.
* bitter smile - 썩소 (썩은 미소)
* take advantage of - 이용하다
* be taken advantage of – 이용당하다

✳ 문법 포인트

여기서 of를 전치사로 보지 않는다.

예 This is the state-of-the-art science. - 이것은 최첨단의 과학이다.
여기서 of를 그저 전치사로 받아들이지 않는 것과 같음.

> * state-of-the-art - 최첨단
> * abusive – 이용하는, 학대하는
> * get by – 연명하다, (사회에서) 살아남다
> * tug (us) around – 휘두르다
> * tug – 잡아당기다
> * get by – 연명하다, (사회에서) 살아남다
> * It makes me angry that I can't say anything. – 아무 말도 못해서 화가 난다. That (접속사)
> * I never have time for either.= I don't have time for both.= 둘 다 할 여유가 없다.
> * be out and about – 밖에 나가 있는, 밖에서 놀고 있는
> * mind off of what is troubling me= 나는 나를 문제 삼는 것들로부터 더 이상 생각하고 싶지 않다.
> * take one's mind off of something – 번뇌를 벗어던지다 (하나에 대한 고민을 떨쳐 버리다)

❋ 친구 Friends

친구들과 자주 싸우는 편은 아니지만 가끔 나도 모르게 혹은 친구도 모르게 나의 민감한 부분에 대해 언급했다가 서로 기분이 나빠질 때가 있는 것 같아.
친구를 위해서 한 말이 친구한테는 상처가 되기도 할 때도 있고 오지랖이 문제라고 해야 할까?
가끔은 서로가 피곤하고 지쳐서 민감할 때 싸울 때도 있기도 하고 말이야.

Although I don't tend to often have arguments with my friends, there are times we hurt each other's feelings because we unintentionally mention some sensitive stuff.

Also, there are times when I say something that I think my friend will like hearing, but it goes the other way. Maybe being nosy can be sometimes a problem?
Moreover, from time to time we have an argument because we both are exhausted from work and at times can be sensitive.

> * have an argument / have arguments 언쟁을 하다, 말다툼을 하다. (Fight은 육체적으로 싸우는 느낌도 있으니 입으로 싸우는 것을 사용할 때는 이 단어를 추천!)
> * hurt one's feelings – 누구의 기분을 상하게 하다.
> * unintentionally - 고의 아니게, 무심코
> * mention - 언급하다
> * sensitive - 민감한
> * stuff - 일, 것(사람들이 일반적으로 행하거나 말하거나 생각하거나 하는 것을 통칭)
> * There are times when I say something that I think my friend will like hearing, but it goes the other way. - 이 말 하면 좋아할 줄 알았는데 (의도치 않게) 아닐 때가 있다
> * nosy - 오지랖, 참견하기 좋아하는 사람
> * moreover - 게다가, 더욱이
> * exhausted - 기진맥진한, 진이 다 빠진, 탈진한
> * at times - 가끔은

* 같은 내용의 다른 문장
Honesty is a problematic aspect of friendship.
I don't tend to argue frequently with my friends, but there are times we hurt each other.
I want to be honest with them, but sometimes honesty hurts. So, is it better to lie?
Sometimes, we forget and mention a sensitive topic from the past. We forget to bite our tongues. By then, it's too late, and the damage is already done.
Our suggestions to each other sometimes hurt too because they

contradict their feelings.
All we are really doing is showing our concerns in a hurtful way inadvertently.
I am thankful for such friends, even when we hurt each other.
At the end of the day, we argue because of these issues, but we care for one another.

* problematic – 문제가 있는, 문제가 많은
* aspect – 측면, 양상
* argue – 언쟁하다, 다투다
* frequently – 자주, 흔히
* bite ones' tongue - 말문이 막히다
* damage is already done – 이미 엎질러졌다, 이미 일이 벌어졌다= spilt milk
* suggestion - 제안, 의견, 제의
* contradict – 모순되게 무엇을 하다
* inadvertently – 의도치 않게

※ 가족 Family

가족이란 참 많이 엉켜버린 실타래 같은 존재이기도 해.
우리가 아무리 좋은 강연과 좋은 말들을 들어도 가족에게 적용하는 것은 참 쉽지 않은 일인 듯해. 소중한 사람을 위해서 잔소리를 하는 가족에게 스트레스를 너무 많이 받기도 하고 너무 가까워서 무신경해질 때도 있지.

Family can be like an entangled thread.
No matter how much seminars you attend and how much positive things you hear from others, applying them to family is never an easy task.
I get my feelings hurt by hearing so much naggings from my family.
Over time, you get used to it and it starts to feel numb at the end.

* entangled thread – 꼬인 실타래
* easy task – 쉬운 일
* nag - 잔소리하다 * nagging – 잔소리
* over time – 시간이 지날수록
* get used to – 익숙해지다
* numb – 마비가 되다(무신경해지다)
* at the end - 끝에는, 나중에는

＊ 같은 내용의 다른 문장

Family can be a thread full of emotional entanglement.
No sweet talk can get you out of the dips and once a feeling is hurt, it will stay hurt until the remedy is applied. Every once in a while, I fall victim to the heinous amount of naggings put forth by those that love me.
Your family ties sometimes can instigate someone to react in such a manner that it will hurt you in the most vulnerable parts in your heart.

> ＊ entanglement - 꼬여 있는 것, 얽힘
> ＊ get you out of the dips - 구덩이에서 빼내다
> ＊ remedy - 치유법, 치유하다
> ＊ fall victim to - 무언가에 피해를 받게 되다
> ＊ heinous= terrible or horrible - 끔찍한
> ＊ nagging - 잔소리
> ＊ put forth by - 무언가에 의해서 진행이 된
> ＊ instigate - 착수하게 하다
> ＊ vulnerable - 취약한

❋ 취업 Looking for a Job

취업한다는 것은 걱정이 한없이 되면서도 설렐 수 있는 말이 아닐까 싶네.
돈을 스스로 번다는 설렘과 강한 성인이 되는 단계 중 하나일 수 있지만 내가 현실과 부딪힐 준비가 되었을까? 하는 두려운 생각을 하기도 하지.
어떤 이들은 정말 최선을 다해 이력서를 100개를 넘게 지원하는 사람도 있는 한편 어디로 갈지 확실치 않아 이력서를 넣지도 못하고 힘들어하기도 하지.
묘한 감정을 주는 일이란 말이야.

I think the thought of getting a job can be worrisome and exciting prospect.
The idea of making money can be a next level excitement and act as

a stepping stone in becoming a real grown-up.
Am I ready to take on the real world? I get doubtful about my own capabilities.
Some people really go out of their ways and submit up to a hundred resumes.
On the other side of spectrum, there are those who just cannot make up their mind and choose the right career paths. This process gives us mixed feelings.

* prospect – 사업, 해야 하는 것, 가망성
* spectrum – 범위, 영역
* on the other side of spectrum= on the other hand - 반면에
* get a job – 취업하다, 직업을 얻다
* worrisome - 걱정스럽게 만드는, 걱정스러운
* make money – 돈을 벌다
* stepping stone - 디딤돌
* grown-up - 큰, 장성한, 어른, 성인이 된
* doubtful - 확신이 없는, 의심을 품은
* capabilities - 능력들, 역량들
* submit – 제출하다
* make up one's mind – 마음을 정하다
* right career paths – 나에게 알맞은 진로들
* mixed feelings – 복잡한 감정

*** 같은 내용의 다른 문장**

I think that the idea of getting a job can cause conflicting emotions. You might be anxious but excited at the same time. Everyone has their reasons that may lead them to feel certain ways. It might be the money, the independence, or being one step closer to becoming a grown-up. Even still, I have my doubts—I'm unsure if I am ready to start working and being on my own. But I have to realize, at some point that I must enter into the same reality as everyone else. I hear of people making all the possible moves that give them the best

chance.
They send out more than 100 resumes in hoping to score any job possible.
On the other hand, there are others who hesitate. They only want to apply to jobs that suit them best. However, I think this process of job-searching exposes just how different people are.

> * cause - ~을 야기하다, 초래하다
> * conflicting emotions – 부딪히는 감정들
> * at the same time - 동시에
> * Everyone has their reasons that may lead them to feel certain ways. - 어떻게 느끼는지는 누구나 다 그들만의 이유가 있다.
> * independence - 독립, 자립
> * a (one) step closer to - 어디에 가깝게 다가가다
> * grown-up _____(위에서 답 찾아보기)
> * doubts - 의심, 의문, 의혹들
> * realize - 깨닫다
> * at some point – 언젠가는
> * reality - 현실
> * score - 점수, 무엇을 얻어내다
> * on the other hand – _____ (위에서 답 찾아보기)
> * hesitate - 망설이다, 주저하다
> * suit – 나에게 맞다
> * job-searching – 일자리 찾기
> * expose - 드러내다, 폭로하다

❋ 성공 Success

성공이란 무엇일까? 성공의 개념을 지을 수 있는 것에는 10가지가 넘는다고 해. 누구는 지위가 높아져야 하며, 누구는 돈을 많이 벌어야 하고, 누구는 좋은 결혼을 하는 것, 누구는 다른 사람들을 도울 수 있는 상태가 되었을 때, 누구는 똑똑해야 하고, 누구는 외모가 될 수도 있고 수많은 것 같아.

꿈을 찾는 삶의 영어

내 스스로 어떤 상태일 때 행복할 수 있을까, 라는 건 사람마다 다르니까.
그 성공이라는 단어는 참 애매한 단어이면서 우리에게 큰 원동력을 주는 단어인 것 같아.
성공이라고 생각한 것을 이루고 허탈한 사람도 있기도 하고, 성공이라는 꿈의 동기부여를 받아 나를 더 좋은 환경으로 만들 수도 있고 매우 철학적인 어려운 단어인 것 같아.

What is success? Some say there are more than ten ways to define the word 'success'.
Some people desire to have elevated status, some desire to earn a lot of money, some desire to be intelligent, some desire to be in a position to be able to help others, and some desire to be good-looking. There are countless other definitions of success.
Everyone has a different idea of what true happiness is, so we define it in our most subjective ways. The word success seems to be a very vague one, yet very motivating word to us.
Some people feel disheartened after achieving what they thought was a success.
The driving force of achieving your dream of success can improve the quality of your life.
Success is a very difficult concept to grasp.

* success _____ (위에서 답 찾아보기)
* desire - 바라다, 원하다
* elevate - 승진시키다, 높이다, 올리다
* status – 신분, 지위
* good-looking - 잘생긴, 보기 좋은
* countless – 무수한, 셀 수 없이 많은
* subjective - 주관적인, 마음속에 존재하는
* vague - 모호한, 애매한
* disheartened - 낙담하게 하다
* achieve - 성취하다

＊ 같은 내용의 다른 문장

What is success? Some say that there are more than ten different ways to define the concept of the word "success." Even still, we all have a concept in our minds of what we associate success with. Some envision an elevated status, some a high income. For others, it is to be highly intelligent, good-looking, and then there are others who seek making a difference outside of their own interest and prioritize the needs of others. Even with these definitions laid out like this, there are undoubtedly countless others.

Yet, the idea of success is different for all of us. Success leads us to independent happiness. Because we all define happiness in a variety of ways, it should come as no surprise that we all have our own ideas of what makes us successful.

Despite the idea of success being vague, it is a very motivating word for us.

Yet, success is not always as it seems. There are people who feel an unexpected sense of despondence after achieving their goals after realizing it was not the success they were seeking. But this is not always the case. There are also many who feel satisfied when they succeed so long as they are honest with themselves.

If you set out to help those of in need and use that as your motivation, we will often feel dissatisfied with what we achieve because the concept of success was never ours to begin with.

Motivation moves us towards success, and because of the dreams we have, we can make a better life for ourselves in the future. Thus, success is a very difficult concept to understand if we do not first understand ourselves.

---

* associate something with - ~을 ~과 관련지어 생각하다
* envision - 큰 그림을 그리다, 큰 꿈을 꾸다= imagine – 상상하다
* elevated status – 상승된 나의 위치(사회적인 위치)
* high income - 높은 수익
* intelligent - 지적인, 지능이 있는

* prioritize - 우선순위를 매기다
* lay out – 펼쳐 놓다(내가 아는 것을 펼쳐 놓다)
* undoubtedly - 의심할 여지없이, 확실히
* countless – _____ (위에서 답 찾아보기)
* in a variety of ways – 다양한 방법으로
* come as no surprise – 놀라움으로 느껴지지 않는다, 놀라움으로 다가오지 않는다
* vague – _____ (위에서 답 찾아보기)
* despondence – 낙심, 의지가 꺾임, 낙담
* seek - 찾다
* this is not always the case – 항상 이렇지만은 않다
* satisfaction - 만족, 흡족
* If you set out to help those of in need and use that as your motivation - 도움이 필요로 하는 사람들을 챙기는 것을 너에 동기 부여로 쓰게 된다면
* never ours to begin with – 애초에 ~가 아니었다
* dissatisfied with - ~에 불만족스러워 하는

4. 평상시 일상
Daily routine

❋ 현재의 내 일상 My Daily Routine

내 일상은 항상 바쁜 편이야.
나 같은 경우는 바쁘게 지내야 정신적으로 편해지는 편이거든.
주변 사람들은 가끔 왜 그렇게 몸을 혹사하냐고 하기도 하는데 이게 나인 걸 뭐 어떡해. 일단 나는 체질적으로 야행성 인간이지만 아침 7시 전에 일어나려고 정말 노력을 많이 하는 편이야. 아침에 일어나서 헬스장에 다녀온 후에 나는 프리랜서로 일을 하고 있어서 스케줄을 먼저 정리해.
그 후 오전 10시쯤이 되면 학생들을 가르치고, 학원에 갔다가 오면 어느새 저녁이 되어 있지.
하루 평균 4-5개 정도 수업이 있는 편이야. 수업이 끝나면 내가 수업을 받기도 하고 책을 읽거나 공부를 하거나 혹은 집에 있는 고양이랑 놀기도 하고 집 청소를 하기도 해.
그리고 최대한 새벽 1시 전에는 자려고 해. 원래 자기 전 맥주 마시는 걸 매우 좋아하는데 간이 안 좋아지면서 술을 덜 마시려고 노력하고 있어.

My daily life always tends to be very hectic.
In my case, I'm kind of a person who takes comfort in keeping myself busy all the time.
People around me often ask why I am so hard on myself.
But, I am who I am.
First of all, I am instinctively a night owl; I tend to make a lot of efforts to wake up before 7 in the morning.
After going to the gym in the morning, I organize my schedule first. This is imperative as I'm working as a freelancer.
After that around 10 a.m., I teach students. After working at the academy, it's already evening.

꿈을 찾는 삶의 영어

I have an average of 4 to 5 classes to teach in a day. After I'm done teaching, I take classes myself too. Then, I read books, study, clean my house or play with my cats at home.
I try to sleep before one am as often as possible.
(학교에서는 and로 시작하지 말라고 하는데 사람들이 몰라서 자주 쓰는 편)
I like to drink beer before I go to bed. However, I'm trying not to drink it as my liver is getting worse.

* instinctively – 본능적으로, 천성적으로, 체질적으로
* tend to – _____ (위에서 답 찾아보기)
* hectic – _____ (위에서 답 찾아보기)
* I'm kind of – 나는 약간
* comfort -위로하다, 위안하다
* hard on somebody- somebody에게 심하게 대하다
  예) Don't be too hard on yourself! – 너를 너무 혹사 시키지 마.
* I am who I am - 나는 나야, 이게 나인걸?
* first of all - 우선
* a night owl – 밤늦게 자는 사람, 올빼미형 인간
* make a lot of efforts - 많은 애를 쓰다
* imperative – 반드시 해야 하는
* freelancer - 프리랜서
* average – 평균의
* as often as possible – 가능한 한 자주
* liver - 간

* 문법 포인트

1. as 형용사(자유롭게 넣어주기) as possible

예문

as much as possible – 되도록 많이
as soon as possible – 되도록 빨리 (soon= 이내, 빨리)
as far as possible – 되도록(가능한) 멀리 (많이, 힘껏)
I want to study as much as possible. (가능한 한 많이 공부를 많이 하고 싶다.)
Scarlett told her she would come as soon as possible. (스칼렛은 그녀

에게 되도록 빨리 오라고 했다.)
Stay away from the racoon as far as possible. (너구리한테서 최대한 멀리 떨어져 있어.)

2. be + getting + 비교급 - 점점 ~해지고 있다.

예문
It is getting colder. – 점점 더 추워지고 있어.
She is getting prettier. – 그녀는 점점 더 예뻐지고 있어.

* 같은 내용의 다른 문장
Some say it's not by choice, but I choose to live a hectic life style.
Maybe it's because, in my case, I feel better when I make myself busy.
I like to stay moving, keep myself active with busy work, and push myself to keep doing more.
People around me often ask me why I am so hard on myself.
They tell me to slow down, but I just can't.
I am who I am.
To start if off, I am naturally a night owl through and through. I've always been this way.
It takes everything to get up before 7 in the morning.
After completing my morning workout routine at the gym, I organize my schedule to avoid a conflict in my schedule. This step is imperative for my day to run without a hitch because I am working as a freelancer now. My success relies solely on me.
When 10 am rolls around, you will find me teaching in the classroom at the academy, and you won't find me leaving the school's grounds until it is already evening.
On average, I teach 4 to 5 classes a day. Yet, this does not alter the path which I'm on to get to where I want to be. I move throughout my day from teaching to taking classes myself. At home, I read, study, commit myself to the chores that have been waiting for me, or busy myself with spending time with my cats, who miss me all

day. And if I am lucky, I try to fall asleep and prepare for tomorrow no later than one am.

But I always feel like I could have done more with my 24 hours than how much I actually complete in a single day. There are some consequences that follow with this type of life style.

Self-medicating by drinking is a bad habit I am prone to repeat.

I like to drink beer before going to bed. However, I'm trying not to drink as my liver is getting worse.

* some - (몇몇 사람들은) 누군가는
* it's not by choice - 내가 원해서 한 것이 아니다
* slow down - ~을 늦추다, 느긋해지다
* to start if off – 시작을 해보자면
* naturally – 당연히, 자연스럽게
* through and through= completely 완전히, 하나부터 열까지[속속들이]
* it takes everything – 혼신을 다해
* routine - 일상, 규칙적으로 하는 일
* conflict - 갈등, 충돌
* imperative – 매우 중요한= crucial
* without a hitch – (without a mistake/hiccup) - 실수 없이
* solely – 완전히 하나에 의해서
* rolls around – 다가왔다
* school's grounds – 학교 범위
* on average - 평균적으로, 대체로
* alter - 변하다, 달라지다, 고치다
* path – 길
* This does not alter the path which I'm on to get to where I want to be. (이것이 내가 가고자 하는 길에 방해를 하지는 않는다.)
* throughout - ~하는 동안에, ~인 동안에
* commit - 저지르다, 범하다
* chores – _____ (위에서 답 찾아보기)
* consequences – (발생한 일의) 결과, 중요함
* I am prone to repeat. – 반복할 경향이 높다

❖ 내 과거의 일상 My Past Routine

나의 과거의 일상이라....
사실 나는 고등학교 때까지는 신기하겠지만 아침에 학교에 등교해서 7교시까지 점심시간을 제외하고 거의 잠을 잔 것 같아.
내가 수업 시간에 일어나 있으면 선생님께서 "저 귀신이 어떻게 일어나 있어?" (머리 때문에 목을 내리고 얼굴을 긴 머리로 가린 채 귀신처럼 잤기 때문이지) 이렇게 놀라실 정도였으니깐. 나는 학교 후 집에 와서 하루 종일 컴퓨터 게임을 하곤 했어.
이러니 학교에서 매일 잠에 빠져 있던 거지.
고등학교 2학년까지는 아무 생각 없이 방황하고 인생이란 무엇일까, 라는 생각과 좀 지루하고 인생이 무의미했던 시절이었던 것 같아.
지금 생각해 보면 참 시간을 낭비했다고 생각하지만 이미 지난 일인 걸 뭐? 그래서 후회하며 뒤를 돌아보려 하지는 않아.

My routine in the past?
To be honest, it might be shocking but, until I was in high school, I used to sleep all day from the morning until the last class. The only exception was lunch time.
On the rare occasion when I was awake in class, teachers would shout out "How is that ghost awake?"(Because I used to put my chin down and sleep, hiding my face with my long hair like a scene from horror movies.)
I used to play computer games all day after school.
That's why I fell asleep every day at school.
Until the second year of high school, I wandered around directionless,
(I felt like I have lost my way) and wondered what life was.
It was a time when life felt a little boring and meaningless to me.
Now thinking back, I wasted a lot of time, but I can't get that time back
So, I no longer dwell on the past.

* to be honest – 솔직히 말해서
* shocking – 충격적인
* exception - 예외적인 것
* on the rare occasion – 가끔씩은
* awake – 깨어 있는, 잠들지 않은
* shout out – 큰소리로 말하다
* chin down – (턱) 고개를 아래로 숙이다
* hide someone's face – 누군가의 얼굴을 숨기다
* scene – 현장, 장면
* that's why + 주어 동사 – 그러한 이유로, 이래서 동사하다.

> 예문

That's why I came late – 그래서 내가 늦은 거야.
This is why Scarlett wrote a book. (이래서 스칼렛이 책을 쓴 거야.)
* wander around directionless – 방향성 없이 맴돌다, 방황하다
* lose one's way - 길을 잃다.
* meaningless - 의미 없는, 무의미한
* think back – 돌이켜 생각해 보다
* waste time – 시간을 낭비하다
* no longer - 더 이상 ~않다, 이미 ~아니다.
* dwell on – 곱씹다, 얽매이다

* 문법 포인트

1. Passed vs past

passed – 육체적인 무엇이 지나갔다.

> 예문

He passed the sign that said 'Barbershop' and thought about getting a haircut. (그는 '이발소'라는 간판을 (보고) 지나치면서 머리를 자를까 하고 생각했다.)
I passed him by at the groceries the other day. (이틀쯤 전에 슈퍼마켓에서 그를 지나쳤다. (봤다))
epast – 형태 없는 것이 (형용적인) 지나가다
It was already past midnight. (이미 자정이 지나버렸다.)
The deadline was already past due. (마감일이 이미 지나 버렸다.)

❋ 내가 바라는 미래의 일상 My Future Routine

내가 바라는 일상은 일단 내가 정말 원하는 보라색 Jeep 차를 하는 거야. 그 차를 운전해 주시는 분이 있으면 좋을 것 같아.

일단 생각을 적는 거니 내 맘대로 비현실적이어도 적어 볼게. 상상하는 건 자유잖아?

아침 5-6시 사이에 일어나서 건강식을 먹고 가끔 운전해 주시는 분의 차를 타고 P.T를 받으러 가서 운동을 한 시간 정도 하고 명상을 하러 가는 거야. 대략 8시까지 운동과 명상을 하고 집에서 샤워를 한 후 메이크업을 받으러 숍으로 가서 준비를 하고 내 학원으로 출근을 하고 직원들과 한 시간 정도 미팅을 하는 거야. 그 후에 책 집필을 하고 학원 자료 연구를 하고, 학원 관리 후에 저녁에는 미국에 있는 학원 매니저와 또 미팅을 나누지. 나는 한두 달에 한 번씩 학원 관리를 위해 미국에 왔다 갔다 하고 있어. 저녁에는 유튜브 영상 아이디어를 연구한 뒤 저녁을 먹고 마사지를 받으러 갔다 와. 그 후 자기 전 오늘 내가 받은 스트레스나 머리를 정리하기 위해 줌으로 심리 상담을 받고 일기를 쓰고 잠에 드는 거야. 상상만 해도 설레는 꿈인 것 같아.

미래 일상만 봐도 하루도 가만 못 있는 성격인 것 알 것 같지 않아?

My dream is that I want to buy a purple jeep. It would be great if I have a driver (chauffeur - 불어). First of all, I'm writing down my thoughts, so I'll write them down even if they're unrealistic. We have the right to imagine without limitation, right?

I wake up between five to six am, have a healthy meal, and ride the car with the driver and I go to the gym to exercise with my personal trainer. After I exercise for about an hour, I would go meditate. Then I would take a shower and go to a salon to get my makeup done.

Next, I would go to work at my own academy and have a staff meeting with my employees for about an hour. Later, I would work on writing my book and develop materials for my academy. I imagine having two meetings. The first meeting would be here in South Korea with my employees. The second would be with managers in L.A. in the evening after managing the academy. I envision myself going back and forth between the United States and South Korea once or twice a month for my business.

In the evening, after browsing through YouTube I contemplate ideas for videos of my own.

Later, I would eat dinner and go get a massage.

Before going to bed, I would have a therapy session via Zoom in order to deal with my stress.

I would write in my journal for a while and fall asleep. It's a dream that makes my heart flutter with anticipation just by imagining it. Just by looking at my imagination of my future diary tells you that I'm a person who can't stay still for a day. If you could envision your future in this way, what would it look like?

---

* a driver - (chauffeur - 불어), 운전자, (부자나 중요 인물의 차를 모는) 기사, 대리인(비서)
* first of all - 가장 먼저, 우선
* unrealistic - 비현실적인
* limitation - 국한, 제약, 한계
* right - 옳은

* imagine – 상상하다
* personal trainer – 개인 트레이너
* meditating - 명상
* salon 상점, 살롱, (보통 미용실, 네일아트 숍 같은 곳에 많이 쓰인다.)
* get one's makeup done – 화장을 하다
* employee - 직원
* work on - ~에 애쓰다, 공들이다
* materials - 자재, 자료들
* envision – _____ (위에서 답 찾아보기)
* back and forth - 왔다 갔다
* browsing through - 살펴보다
* contemplate - (어떤 일의 발생 가능성을) 생각하다[예상하다]
* therapy session - 세러피 시간
* journal - 일기(특히 아이들은 diary로 많이 쓰지만 어른들은 journal이라고 많이 쓴다)
* That makes my heart flutter with anticipation. – 그것이 기대감 속에서 설레게 만들다.
* anticipation - 기대
* stay still – 가만히 있다.

* **내 이름 : _____ 바라는 미래의 일상 적어 보기**
(Write about your ideal future routines.)

* 같은 내용의 다른 문장

When I peak into the future, the future I have created, I want to see a little purple Jeep in it. The Jeep Wrangler is perfect for traveling in my opinion.

I can go as wild as I want to since I'm only imagining things in my head. No reason not to go wild, am I correct?

I know that that's too far in the future for now and how unrealistic it sounds.

Be that as it may, I might not accomplish them all but I want to see what my dreams truly are. We have the right to dream without limitation, right?

Every day now, I wake up between five to six am, have a healthy meal, go to the gym and leave for my usual meditation sessions.

After my morning routine is done at around eight am, I go to my academy and have a meeting with employees for about an hour and fulfil my role. I cram in as much as I can during the first couple hours during my day.

Let's fast forward to my evenings. I work on writing my books, do my research for study materials, take care of the business in relation to my academy, and I would have a Zoom meeting with my foreign manager for an overseas branch. I frequently visit USA for the management purposes to keep the things running smooth.

After studying YouTube videos for ideas, I eat dinner and pay off the day's hard work with a massage. Before going to bed, to complete my day, I have a counseling session with my psychologist through Zoom to discuss my issues and sort out any unnecessary lingering thoughts. Then, I write in my journal and drift off to sleep.

A dream that makes my heart flutter just by thinking about it. Just looking into my imagination gives you the sense that I am a person that can't stay still, right?

* peak into the future – 미래를 들여다보다
* go wild (in my head) – 상상을 해 보다
* be that as it may - 그렇다 하더라도
* fulfil my role – 내 역할을 충실히 이행해 내다
* cram in - 한꺼번에 다 하다, 한 군데에 다 집어넣다
* cram – 몰아넣다
* in relation to – 그것에 관한
* let's fast forward to something – 시간을 거기까지 빨리 돌리자
* pay off – 보상하다
* drift off – (피상적으로) 어딘가로 떠나가다
* drift off to sleep - 잠이 들다
* counseling session – 상담
* sort out - 분류하다, 문제를 해결하다
* unnecessary - 불필요한
* lingering thoughts – 맴도는 생각들
* overseas branch - 해외 지점
* frequently - 자주, 흔히
* purpose – 목적, 의도
* make one's heart flutter - 누구를 설레게 하다

스칼렛의
삶 이야기
Scarlett's
Life Story

1. When was a time when you were the happiest?
넌 가장 행복했을 때가 언제야?

내가 가장 행복할 때는 물론 내가 좋아하는 것들을 할 때겠지?
나는 깊이 생각해 보면 내가 좋아하는 친구들과 좋은 시간을 보낼 때, 내가 가르치는 학생들에게 도움이 되는 느낌을 받을 때, 내가 무언가를 열심히 해서 성취할 때, 예를 들면 시험을 봤을 때 잘 본다거나 내 사업이 잘 된다거나, 남으로부터 진심 어린 칭찬을 받을 때, 난 그리고 좀 특이하게 남들에게 관심을 받을 때 행복한 감정이 들기도 하는 것 같아.
아, 그리고 마사지를 받을 때. '아... 내가 이러려고 돈을 버는구나." 자주 생각할 때도 있어.
친구들이랑 호캉스 갈 때도 행복하고 내가 키우는 새끼 고양이를 보고 있을 때도 행복하고 내가 행복할 수 있는 일들이 참 많네?

Of course, I'm the happiest when I'm doing the things that I love, right?
If you think about it deeply, the true happiness comes from being with people you love, like your friends for instance. Personally I feel happy when I provide help for my students and when I achieve something by working hard. For example, when I take an exam, I get good results, I do well in my business, or get sincere compliments from others.
Some people might hate it, but I sometimes enjoy getting attention from others.
Additionally, when I get a massage, I often think, "Oh, this is why I work so hard."
I'm happy when I have a staycation with my friends, and also, I'm happy when I see my kittens playing on their own.
There are so many thing I can be grateful for, see?

* for instance - 예를 들어
* personally - 개인적으로
* compliment - 찬사, 칭찬
* get attention - 주의를 끌다
* additionally - 게다가
* staycation - (신조어 요즘 사람들이 많이 쓰는) 호캉스
* kitten - 새끼 고양이

* 같은 내용의 다른 문장

Of course, we can all say that the happiest times in our lives are when we are doing what we find enjoyable, right?
Think deeply. What makes you happy? Is there a certain time when? For me, it's when I am having a good time with my friends.
When I feel like my students are growing. Or when I feel that I have achieved something that I can be proud of. For example, when I pass an exam with good marks, success in business, or receive sincere compliments from others. Although, I think that this last observation is pretty normal. I can't imagine that there are too many people who would be unhappy with a compliment, so long as it is genuine.
I also find happiness when I do things to relieve stress. When I get a massage and all my worries slip away, I think to myself, "Oh! This is what I earn money for!"
Other things that lift my heart are simple. They don't have to be extravagant.
A staycation with my friends or watching my kittens play.
We don't need a lot to make ourselves happy so long as there is personal meaning behind it.
The more I think, the more I realize how much of my life brings a smile to my face.
But enough about me, we should put ourselves in more positive situations and mindsets!

- good marks – 좋은 점수: good scores
- observation – 관찰 사항
- so long as it is genuine – 진실하기만 한다면
- I can't imagine - 상상을 할 수 없다
- that there are too many people - 많은 사람들이 있을 거라고는
- who would be unhappy with a compliment? - 칭찬을 들어도 행복하지 않은 사람이 있을까?
- slip away – 손아귀에서 벗어나다, 내가 어떻게 할 수 없다
- extravagant – 굉장한, 화려한, 사치스러운= Special x 2의 느낌
- lift my heart – 내 마음을 치유해 준다(마음의 짐을 덜어 줌)
- so long as there is personal meaning behind it – 개인적으로 의미가 있다면
- mindset - 마음가짐

❈ 스칼렛의 삶 이야기 Scarlett's Life Story

나는 서울에서 태어나 매우 에너지 넘치고 말괄량이로 자라 왔어. 초등학교 6학년쯤 신도시인 남양주로 이사를 가게 되었고 6학년부터 중, 고등학교까지 친구도 많고 사고도 많이 치고, 장난기도 많고, 매우 씩씩한 아이였지만 항상 뭔가 공허한 게 많았던 것 같아. 중학교 때는 "인생은 뭘까?"라는 생각도 많이 했고 학교에서는 거짓말 안 하고 1교시부터 점심시간을 제외하고는 잠을 잘 때가 많았지. 심지어 수업 시간에 잠을 자고 있지 않으면 선생님께서 안 잔다고 신기해하신 적도 있었지.

그러다가 고3쯤이 되어서 현실과 맞닿게 되었던 것 같아.

"내가 하고 싶은 게 뭐지?" "나는 뭘 해야 하지?"라는 생각에 곰곰이 빠져 있기도 하고, 공부를 정말 열심히 하는 짝꿍에게 "너는 왜 열심히 공부해?"라는 질문을 던져 보기도 하고, 매일 밤을 울며 우울증에 빠지기도 했어. 그러던 어느 날 스페인어 선생님께서 추천한 한 자기 계발서인 박현우 작가의 《대한민국 20대 일찍 도전하라》를 읽고 충격을 받게 돼.

여기서 저자가 하루에 3-4시간을 잔다고 하는데 그때 그 문구를 읽고 "내가 하루 자는 시간에 이 사람은 3-4일 이상 깨어 있는 건가?" 하고 머리를 퉁 맞은 것 같은 느낌이 들었어.

그 책을 읽고 난 뒤 나는 꿈을 크게 꿔야겠다는 생각을 했어. 그 저자가 너무 멋져 보였고 세계적으로 유명한 사람이 돼야겠다는 생각으로 하루에 14시간씩, 스톱워치를 켜놓고 영어를 공부하게 돼. 고3이었지만 파닉스도 잘 몰랐었는데, 1년 반 뒤에는 성인들 영어 회화 과외를 시작하고 5년 뒤 캐나다 유학을 가서 대학을 졸업하고 9년 뒤 성인 영어로 사업자 등록을 내게 되지. 그 중간중간 호주로 워킹홀리데이도 다녀오고 대치동에서 학생들 강의와 강남에서 성인 어학원에서 영어 회화를 가르치기도 했어. 10년 뒤 성인 어학원을 차리고 미국에서도 할 사업에 꿈을 향해 달려가고 있는 중이야. 내가 말하고 싶은 것은, 정말 열정과 노력이 있다면, 영어에 옳은 교육법을 찾을 수 있고, 제대로 된 영어를 할 수 있다고 생각해. 같이 힘내자!

I was born and raised in Seoul. I went to a local elementary school here.
I was very energetic and kind of a boisterous girl.
I moved to Namyangju, a new town, when I was in 6th grade and

went to middle and high school there.
I had a lot of friends. We were always making trouble.
I was a playful and brave child. However, I think I used to feel that there were always a lot of void in my life. When I was in middle school, I often asked myself the question, "What is the meaning of life?" At school, to be honest, I used to sleep all day long except during lunchtime
There was even a time when my teacher would be surprised if I wasn't sleeping in class.
Then, when I became a senior in high school, I was starting to face the reality.
I had questions that used to linger in my head such as, "What do I want to do in my life?", "What should I do in the future?"
I used to think about those questions over and over again.
Moreover, I used to ask questions to my desk-mate who studied really hard.
"Why do you study so hard?"
Unfortunately, I used to weep every night and ended up falling into depression.
Then one day, I was shocked when I read a book called 《Challenge Early in your 20s》 by Park Hyun-woo, a self - help book recommended by my Spanish teacher.
The author said he sleeps three to four hours a day in the book. When I read this part, I felt like somebody had hit me on the head, saying, "Do I sleep five times the amount of hours in a day compared to him?" because I used to sleep for 15 hours per day.
After reading the book, I decided to dream big. The author seemed so cool.
With the idea of becoming an globally famous person in mind, I started studying English for 14 hours a day with a timer on even.
Even though I was a senior in high school, I was barely trained in phonics. But a year and a half later, I started tutoring Conversational English for adults.

Five years later, I went to Canada as an international student and graduated from college. When I returned to Korea, I registered for a business license to acquire the credentials to teach English to adults.
Before registering for my license, I went to Australia to work overseas, Koreans know this as Working Holiday.
After coming back, I taught students in Daechi-dong, and I taught Conversational English at an adult language academy in Gangnam.
Now, my dream is to establish adult language academies in 10 years and run a business in the United States as well. I believe if you have the right type of passion, willingness to put in the efforts, then you will be able to find the learning method that works for you which will allow you to speak English fluently.

* local elementary school - 동네 초등학교
* energetic - 활동적인
* boisterous - 활동적인, 잠시도 가만히 있지 못하는
* void - 비어 있는
* face the reality - 현실과 맞닥뜨리다
* linger - 남다, 오래 머물러 있다
* desk-mate - (옆자리) 짝꿍
* unfortunately - 불행하게도, 유감스럽게도
* weep - 펑펑 울다
* end up + ing – 결국 ing 하게 되다
* depression - 우울함, 암울함, 우울증
* author - 저자
* hit someone on the head – 깨닫게 해주다
* compared to - ~와 비교하여
* globally - 세계적으로
* barely - 간신히, 가까스로
* phonics - 파닉스, 발음 중심 어학교 수법
* register for - ~에 등록하다
* business license - 사업허가증
* credentials - 자격

> * establish - 설립하다, 수립하다, 확고히 하다
> * run a business - 사업을 운영하다
> * put in the efforts - 노력을 기울이다

* **같은 내용의 다른 문장**

Born in Seoul, I spent my elementary school years in the capital, growing up to be quite the tomboy. I was so energetic and curious back then, even if I was a little defiant.

In 6th grade, I moved to Namyangju, a new town but still the same me. I went to middle school there, made a lot of friends, and ended up in all sorts of trouble. Yet, I think it was my personality that made things turn out this way.

I kept feeling like something was missing in my life. Even back then, I wanted something without knowing what that something was.

I might have been a playful child and very brave, but I always felt like others could not see that I was searching for something that I could not give a name to.

When I was in middle school, my thoughts trailed to the question, "what is life?" It was a question without a meaningful answer for me. Everyone answers for themselves, you know? But my question had no answer. I slept all day at school. I only woke up for lunch and to go home. I didn't want to be part of a world where I could not find the meaning.

On the rare occasion that I was not sleeping in class, I was never awarded positive acknowledgment from my teachers. They would make their comments about me being a ghost, express their surprise, and carry on with the class.

They didn't care. And neither did I. I was not able to face the reality until I entered the senior year in high school.

That question, "What is life?" had manifested into several new and intimidating questions. "What do I want to do?", "What should I do?" They used to tumble about in my mind without an answer. I saw everyone else finding their place. Planning out their future. Studying for exams. But not me. I was a compass without a needle. I felt lost and alone.

> * in the capital – 수도권 안에서
> * back then – 그때는
> * tomboy - 남자 같은 여자
> * defiant – 거역하는, 말 안 듣는 (아이, 사람)
> * turn out this way - 이렇게 됐다
> * can't give a name to something – 생각이 잘 안 난다, 잘 모르겠다.
>   = cannot figure out
> * thoughts trailed to – 생각이 ~로 이어졌다.
> * on the rare occasion – _____ (위에서 답 찾아보기)
> * awarded - 상 받은, 상 받았다
> * acknowledgment – 인정
> * comments - 논평, 언급
> * carry on with - ~을 계속하다.
> * manifested into something – 무언가로 실현이 되다, (무엇이)만들어지게 되다
> * intimidating questions – 두려운 질문들
> * tumble about – 비틀거리다, 우왕좌왕하다, 뒤죽박죽하게 하다
> * compass without a needle – 바늘 없는 나침반, 방향성을 잃은 무엇(미래 계획 없이 방황하는)

* 같은 내용의 다른 문장

I asked other students why they did what they did. Where have they found those much needed directions when I couldn't find mine? I remember asking a classmate who always had it figured out. "Why do you study so hard?" It didn't make sense. I don't know if I just couldn't see it or didn't want to see it. Maybe I just wanted to rebel against what was expected of me.

I used to cry every night back then. I fell into a deep depression. Then, one day, out of the blue, Hyun-woo, Park's 《Challenge Early in your 20s》 caught me by surprise. My Spanish teacher had recommended the book to me, and I quickly started reflecting on each page. The author claimed that he slept three to four hours a day, but as I read this, I began to self-reflect. I felt that someone had slapped me on the wrist, "You mean to say that this person is awake for three to four more days in a week than I am?" because I used to sleep away 15 hours of my day and do little else. It's funny to think of how a book can change your life. I had always heard people saying that something always inspired them without giving their claim much thought.

And here I was with a book in my hand, now thinking about my future. I reevaluated my lifestyle by comparing what I was doing to the author of this book and began to dream big. "What would I need to do to become like him?" "How much of my life would I need to change?", "Where would I even start?" The questions in my mind quickly changed. I felt my life gaining purpose because I decided to give it one.

Having motivation was never something I had experienced before. It was both refreshing and demanding. I started studying English for 14 hours a day with a stopwatch on, just to ensure that I was completing what I said I was going to do for the day. I had a goal now. I had an idea of who I wanted to be, and it drove me forward.

Everything from there moved quickly. I went from being a high schooler who didn't know phonics very well, but a year and a half later, I began tutoring Conversational English for adults. Another five years after that, I went to Canada as an international student and graduated from the local college, registered for a business license as an adult English educator all within the span of nine years' time.

In the meantime, I went to Australia for a Working-Holiday. After coming back, I taught students in Daechi-dong, taught Conversational English at an adult language academy in Gangnam. I have set up my goal for the next 10 years of starting my own adult language academies and to run a business in the United States concurrently.

If you are really passionate and your goal is truly be able to speak English fluently, you have to put in the efforts. And not only that, you have to have the right learning method. Otherwise, your dream will just be a pipe dream. Nothing can stop you!

* out of the blue - 갑자기, 난데없이, 뜬금없이
* claim - 주장하다, 요구하다
* self-reflect – 자아 성찰
* rebel against - ~에 거스르다 동의어: defy : 거역하다
* I just wanted to rebel against what was expected of me. - 나에게 기대하는 것에 거역하고 반대되는 길을 걸었다.
* do little else – do very little – 조금만 하는(이뤄내지 못하는)
* slap someone on the wrist – (현실을 자각하게) 꼬집어 주다
* without giving their claim much thought – 다른 사람에 의견에 의미 부여를 하지 않았다.
* it drove me forward – 나를 앞으로 나아가게 해 주었다.
* high schooler – 고등학생(고딩)
* tutoring - 과외, 개인 교습
* concurrently – 동시에: at the same time
* all within the span of nine years' time - 9년이라는 기간 안에
* in the meantime= in the meanwhile: 그 동안에
* pipe dream - 말도 안 되는 꿈, 허황된 꿈
* pipe 중간에 텅 비어 있기에
* set up – 준비하다
* otherwise - 그렇지 않으면
* nothing can stop you - 아무것도 당신을 멈출 수 없어요

IV

넌 목표와 꿈이 뭐야?
What are your goals and dreams?

1. 내 꿈과 목표는...
My dreams and goals are...

나의 꿈은 앞에서 몇몇 부분은 언급을 했지만 두 가지로 나눌 수 있다고 생각해. 눈에 보이는 것 눈에 보이지 않는 것.
눈에 보이는 것에는 미국과 한국을 왔다 갔다 하며 사업을 하는 것이고 눈에 보이지 않는 것은 남을 도울 때 정말 감사함과 행복함으로 도울 수 있을 만큼의 여유와 많은 이에게 도움과 힘이 되는 사람, 누군가에게 닮고 싶은 사람이 되는 것이야.

I mentioned some of my dreams earlier, I think we can divide it into two categories.
Things that are visible and things that are invisible.
What is tangible is what you can see. It is what is visible to others, such as traveling back and forth between the U.S. and Korea for my business.
What is not tangible, are the things that we cannot hold in our hands, such as the feelings we feel—the feelings we share. When you help others, you feel accomplishment and happiness. Others can see the action, but not the emotions behind the action. But these feelings behind the action are important to me. It connects us to one another. Through gratitude and commitment, we create happiness together.
I want to be the type of person that supports someone to reach their goals, to become a role model. I also want to be abundantly rich in positivity, even if they are not visible for others to see.

* divide it into - ~으로 나누다
* categories - 카테고리, 범주, 종류, 등급
* visible – (눈에) 보이는

* invisible – (눈에) 보이지 않는
* tangible - 만질[감지할] 수 있는, 분명히 실재하는[보이는]
* commitment – 헌신
* accomplishment - 업적
* abundantly - 풍부하게, 풍족하게
* connect - 연결하다
* gratitude - 고마움, 감사
* reach - ~에 이르다

* **같은 내용의 다른 문장**

Earlier, I mentioned some of my dreams.
We can take my dreams and put them into two different spectrums.
The things that are tangible and the things are intangible.
What is going to be for the world to see is my endeavors of being a globe-trotting business owner reaching to places both in the US and South Korea. What the world will be blind to is the amount of gratitude and happiness in my emotions whenever I get to help others that are in need. I hope to be a person who will be on the giving end of the things, be a stepping stone, and a worthy role model for people.

* two different spectrums – 두 가지의 다른 면(들)= categories & sides
* endeavors – (중요한) 도전, 거사(중대한 일)
* globe-trotting – 지구 여기저기를 돌아다니는
* blind – 보지 못하는
* what the world will be blind to is – 세상이 보지 못하는 것은
* in need – 도움이 필요한
* be on the giving end of something – 무언가를 주는 입장에서
* stepping stone – 디딤돌
* worthy – 가치가 있는

V
뜬금없지만 감사함으로 마무리하기!
J

뜬금없지만 감사함으로 마무리하기! J

사실 책을 보면 나는 관심이 없는 사람들에게 저자가 감사함으로 가득 채운 글을 보며 휙휙 넘기곤 했는데 왜 그런지 알 것 같아. 글을 적다 보면 나에게 무수한 사람들이 도움을 줬었다는 걸 깨닫게 되거든. 나의 모든 멘토, 친구, 가족들에게 짧은 감사 노트를 쓰고 싶어.

In fact, when I was reading a book, I used to flip past (skipped) the dedication pages, those filled with gratitude to people whom I was not interested in.
But I now realize why a number of authors write those pages of gratitude.
As I'm writing this down, I'm realizing that countless people have helped me.
I want to write a short thank-you note to all of my mentors, friends and family.

> * flip past – 그냥 넘기는(책 페이지를 대충 보고 넘기는)
> * dedication pages – 책 속에 도와 준 사람들을 적어 놓은 페이지
> * gratitude – _____ (위에서 답 찾아보기)
> * countless – _____ (위에서 답 찾아보기)
> * thank-you note – 감사 글 (감사 편지)

* **같은 내용의 다른 문장**
I think it's interesting to see how much I have changed. When I used to read books, I used to skip past the first pages of a book of which the author dedicated their work to. Maybe I just didn't get the point. The gratitude from the writers of the book didn't mean anything to

me, so it never made an impression. Then, as I started writing my own book, I realized that thanking those that helped you along the way is nothing but normal. It made me stop and think.

I realized how many people have helped me get to where I am today. So, because I now realize that they are just as much a part of any success as the person who is the tip of the spear. I want to leave a short note to thank all of my mentors, my friends, and family for sticking with me. For giving me courage when I had none. And for lending an ear when I needed one most. Thank you for always being there for me. I could have never done it without you all.

* skip past – (무언가를) 지나쳐서 넘어가다
* along the way – (무엇을) 하는 도중에, 동안에
* didn't get the point – 그 부분을 이해하지 못했다
* make an impression – 인상을 남기다
* nothing but normal – 지극히 정상인
* help someone along the way – (어떤 과정 속에서) 누군가를 도와서 같이 가는 과정(way= 과정, along= 같이 가는)
* tip of the spear – 앞장서서 무엇을 하는 사람
* sticking with someone – 누군가의 옆에서 떠나지 않는 (견디다, 버티다)
* give me courage when I had none - 용기가 없을 때 용기를 불어넣어 주다.
* lending an ear – 내 말을 들어주는(lend an ear to someone - 내 말을 들어주다)
* I could have never done. - 못했을 것이다
* without these people – 이 사람들의 (도움) 없이는

9살 어린 동생이지만 나보다 더 오래 산 것처럼 깜짝 놀라는 좋은 말들을 해 주고 항상 최선을 다해 노력하는 내 동생 은영아. 언니는 네 언니여서, 네가 나의 동생이어서 너무 감사하고 사랑한다. 말로 다 표현할 수는 없지만 너를 누구보다도 세상에서 사랑하는 사람 중에 하나라고 자신감 있게 말할 수 있을 거야. 항상 응원하고 네가 어떤 결정을 해도 언니는 너의 편이라는 것을 잊지 마. ☺

Although my sister is 9 years younger than I am, she often surprises me with her wisdom.
(She is wise beyond her years. And she is definitely an old soul lol.)
My sister, Eunyoung, always tries her best.
As an older sister to you, I am deeply grateful for you and love you sincerely my dear sister.
My feelings for you are ineffable, but I think I can confidently say that I am one of the people who love you more than anyone else in the world.
I will always root for you, and please don't forget that no matter what you decide, I will always support you.

> * she is wise beyond her years. – 그녀는 나이에 비해서 성숙하다, 현명하다
> * old soul – 애늙은이
> * root for someone – 누군가를 응원하다
> * support - 지지하다
> * ineffable: immovable – 움직일 수 없는, 평생 변하지 않는

* **같은 내용의 다른 문장**

Although my sister is nine years younger than I am, she often expresses wisdom beyond her years. I think that she is an old soul, ready to give all her knowledge to who are willing to listen. I often feel as though she has lived longer than I have and am surprised by her insights.
To my sister, Eunyoung, who always tries her best, we are family, and I am grateful for that.
I am so appreciative for all the ways you have helped me over the years, the advice and motivation you have given me. Yet, I have trouble putting all of these feelings into words.
I love you, yet even these words seem too simple to express how I feel.
Nonetheless, with confidence, I can claim that out of all the billions of people in the world,

I am one that loves you the most.
Just as you were there for me, I want to be there for you.
Even if you feel the world is against you, just remember, as your big sister, I will forever stand at your side.

> * I have trouble putting all of these feelings into words. – 이러한 감정들을 어떻게 말로 표현해야 할지 모르겠다.
> * put into words – 말로 표현하다
> * give all one's something to – 다 퍼주다
> * be willing to – 기꺼이 ~하다
> * as though - ~인 것 같은 (as if though로 많이 쓰임)
> * appreciative - 고마워하는, 감사하는
> * too ~ to 동사 - 너무 ~해서 (to 뒤) 동사를 못하다
> * nonetheless - 어찌 되었든
> * even if you feel the world is against you – 세상이 너를 등질지라도
> * stand at someone's side – 당신에 곁에 남아 있다, ~의 편을 들다

다산, 집접 포쉬네일 사장님 지은이, 항상 내 편이 되어주는 수진이, 엉뚱하고 발랄한 남아프리카 친구 태스민, 나의 에너자이저 유나, 캐나다에서 열심히 나아가고 있는 나의 소중한 친구 쌍둥이 예지, 예슬이 항상 큰 힘이 되어주고 멋진 사업가가 되어가고 있는 우리 희영이 너희들이 없는 삶은 상상할 수도 없을 것 같아. 너희들과 같이 쌓은 추억으로 나를 더 단단한 사람으로 만들어 주는 것 같구나. 사랑한다.

To Jieun, who runs two nail salons in two cities in Korea, Sujin, who is always on my side, Tasmin, a goofy South African friend, Yuna, my energizer, and my twin friends Emily and Ellen Kim who are working hard in Canada, and lastly but definitely not the least, my soul friend Hee Young who has become an amazing entrepreneur. I can't imagine life without you guys.
It seems that the memories built with your love make me a stronger person. I love you.

* nail salons - 네일샵(들)
* be on one's side – 누구의 옆에서 있어 주다, 누구의 편이 되어 주다
* goofy – 엉뚱한
* energizer – 에너지 넘치는 사람
* lastly but definitely not the least – 마지막으로 절대 소홀히 할 수 없는
* entrepreneur - 사업가

* 같은 내용의 다른 문장

My list of supporters does not stop there. I want to thank, Jieun, who I don't know how she does it but runs two nail salons in two cities. Sujin, who has had enough patience to stick with me over the years. My goofy South African friend Tasmin. My energizer Yuna. And my friends, who are twins, Emily and Ellen Kim, who are all working hard in Canada right now. Lastly, I cannot forget about my soulmate Hee Young who has become an unbelievable entrepreneur in her own rights. I can't imagine life without any of you or where my life would be if you never entered it.

My life would be so empty without all the memories I built with each one of you.

Every moment I have spent with all of you has built me into a stronger person.

I love all of you, and no matter where you are in the world, you will always have a place in my heart even if it is from across an ocean.

* my list of supporters – 나를 도와주는 사람들의 목록
* stick with (me) – 내 곁에서 남아주다, 버텨주다
* unbelievable – 믿기지 않는
* in one's own rights – 내 방식대로

She has successfully established her business in her own rights.
(남들이 안 된다고 할 때)그녀는 그녀의 주관대로 사업을 성공적으로 해냈다.

* establish – 설립하다, 회사를 차리다
* across an ocean – 바다를 건너서

꿈을 찾는 삶의 영어

20대 초반 형용사와 동사도 구분 못하고 철없던 저를 사랑으로 저의 인생을 바꿔준 남양주 프렌즈 어학원 선생님 Jen, Jolean, Stacy 그리고 Sam 선생님들께 감사함을 나누고 싶습니다.

I would like to express my gratitude to teachers Jen, Jolean, Stacy and Sam at Namyangju Friends Language Academy. You taught me with lots of love, and that has changed my life.
Thinking back, it is funny. I was a very immature young girl who had no idea how to distinguish between adjectives and verbs in my early 20s.

* immature - 미숙한
* distinguish - 구별하다

＊ 같은 내용의 다른 문장
Now for my teachers. I want to express my eternal gratitude to Jen, Jolean, Stacy, and Sam at Namyangju Friends Language Academy for their patience with me. Without you, I would have never grown from the immature girl who attended your classes. At the time, I could not distinguish between adjectives and verbs even though I was in my early 20s. You set me straight and put me back on track towards a career that I can be proud of. From the bottom of my heart, thank you.

* eternal - 영원한, 끊임없는
* attend - 참여하다
* set someone straight - 누군가를 잘 적응하게 해주다, 잘 이끌어 주다
* put me back on track - 나를 다시금 올바른 길로 가게 하다
* from the bottom of one's heart - 진심으로 (마음을 다 담아서)

Jen: 진심으로 학생들을 사랑하고 매 수업 매우 솔직한 인생 이야기를 나눠 주시고 열정을 쏟으시는 프렌즈 어학원의 다람쥐 여왕님. 항상 저에게 자비로운 마음, 진심으로 솔직한 조언과 격려들을 해 주셨던 것에 감사합니다.

선생님의 항상 진심 어린 사랑은 학생들로 하여금 큰 힘을 주고 그 사랑을 느낄 수 있었던 것 같습니다.

Jen: Queen Squirrel of Friends Language Academy, who sincerely loves students, shares candid life stories in every class, and pours her passion into it.
Thank you for your empathy and your honesty you showed to me.
And thank you for your advice and encouragement.
I think your students felt your sincere love and it gave them great strength.

> * candid – 매우 개인적인, 사적인, 솔직한
> * pour into - ~를 ~에 퍼붓다
> * empathy – 공감한 후에 느끼는 자비심
> * encouragement – 격려
> * great strength – 큰 힘, 강한 원동력

* 같은 내용의 다른 문장
The Queen Squirrel of Friends Language Academy, who sincerely loves all of her students, shares stories of her life with every class, and pours all of her passion into seeing students thrive. I want to sincerely thank you for all of the honest advice and encouragement you offered me with such an empathetic heart. I could not have done it without your patient nature. I understand that teaching is not just something we do to the mind. It is something that affects the heart. I see that now. You showed me that offering a student love and support will make them strong and that strength will carry them on throughout their life, once a teacher's compassion has entered their hearts.

> * thrive – 번영하다, 잘하다, 번성
> * an empathetic heart – 자비로운 마음
> * patient nature – 천성적인 차분함

> * I understand that teaching is not just something we do to the mind. – 가르치는 것이 그저 주입식으로 하는 것이 아니라는 것을 이해한다.
> * It is something that affects the heart. - 진실된 교육은 마음을 울리는 것이다. (여기서 it은 teaching을 가리킴)
> * will carry them on throughout their life – 삶에서 이끌어 줄 것이다.
> * once a teacher's compassion has entered their hearts. 선생님의 진심이 학생들의 마음을 울렸을 때
> * compassion – 진심, 연민(x) (진심에서 나오는 긍정적인 느낌)

Jolean: 세상에 이렇게 밝고 에너지 넘치는 사람이 있을까 싶은 우리 Jolean 선생님.
늘 긍정적인 에너지와 생각지 못한 따뜻한 격려들로 인해 많은 위로와 힘을 받았습니다.
미소천사, 뇌섹녀, 신비로움의 이미지의 선생님으로 많은 것을 배웠습니다. ☺

Jolean: I wonder if there is anyone more bright and energetic in the world than she is.
I was always comforted by your positive energy and unexpected warm encouragement.
I learned a lot from you, Jolean. You have inspired me with your charismatic teaching style, which is synergized by your bright smile, your intelligent mind, and the mysterious side that exudes out from you naturally.

> * comfort – 위로하다
> * unexpected – 예기치 않은
> * warm encouragement – 따뜻한 격려
> * intelligent mind – 지적인 (마음)사람, 지적인 생각을 가진 사람, 뇌섹녀
> * mysterious – 신비한, 비밀스러운
> * charismatic – 카리스마가 있는
> * synergized – 시너지 효과를 발휘하는
> * exudes out – 아우라가 느껴지는, 아우라가 있는
> * naturally – 자연스럽게

* 같은 내용의 다른 문장

Jolean: I wonder if there is anyone as bright and energetic in the world like you. Your positive influence and unexpected inexhaustible warm encouragement always got me up.
and going again. You never tired of cheering me on, and you never got sick of giving me your motivating pep talks.
You are like my guardian angel that will never let me fall far before offering me your hand to get back up and try again. Your bright smile is contagious. I can never seem to keep a frown around you. I've learned so much from your beautifully created intelligent mind.
You are a mysterious teacher. You always know what I need to hear, and show me how I can use what I've learned from my mistakes and use it as a way to motivate me towards my goals.

---

* inexhaustible – 지칠 수가 없는, 바닥이 보이지 않는
* get one up – 누구를 다시 일어설 수 있게 하다, 버팀목이 되어주다
* cheer on - ~을 응원하다
* pep –talk – 격려[응원] 연설
* guardian angel – 수호천사
* offer - 제공하다
* offer one's hand to get back up and try again – 누군가에게 손을 내밀어 다시 일어설 수 있게 하다
* contagious – 전염성이 있는
* frown – 얼굴을 찡그리는

Stacey: 차도녀 같지만 그 안에서 느껴지는 선생님의 학생과 영어에 대한 사랑은 학생들도 다 알고 있을 듯합니다. "영어 선생님들은 학생들을 위해 완벽주의자가 되어야 한다"라고 수업 시간에 툭 던진 말은 잊지 않고 늘 학생들에게 옳은 수업을 하기 위해 노력할 수 있는 좋은 말씀들 많이 나눠 주셔서 감사합니다. J

Stacey: I still remember what you said in class: "In order to be an English teacher, we should be a perfectionist for students". I want to say thank you for always sharing good advice with us.

I always try to remember what you said and teach my students accordingly.
I felt like you were a city girl. But I think all the students felt you were warm and full of love. All the students could feel how passionate you were about teaching English.

- * perfectionist – 완벽주의자
- * accordingly – 그에 맞춰, 그런 이유로
- * city girl - 도시 여자, 도시녀
- * passionate - 열정적인

* **같은 내용의 다른 문장**

Stacey: When we met, I felt like you were a city woman. I realize that first impressions can be wrong sometimes. All the students felt your love, even if you did not outwardly express it. Your passion for teaching students English came through your action and dedication. I still remember what you said in class, "in order to be an English teacher, we must be perfectionists for the sake of our students, I agree. You expressed many wise things to us. I want to thank you for everything your approach, your words, and your motivation. I feel like this list of what I am grateful for from learning from you could go on for a while. I think of what you said often. I always try to remember what you said and use the right methods to ensure my students have the best education I can offer them.

- * first impressions – 첫 인상
- * outwardly - 표면적으로, 겉으로 보이게끔
- * for the sake of our students – 학생들을 위해서 (sake: 어떠한 사람을 위해 무엇을 하는 이유)
- * for one's sake - ~위해서
- * express - 표현하다
- * approach - 접근하다, 다가가다.
- * could go on for a while – 꽤 오랫동안 ~이 지속될 것이다.
- * ensure - 보장하다, 반드시 ~하게 하다.

Sam: 옆집 언니 같은 따뜻함과 정말 언니같이 진심으로 고민이나 힘든 점을 잘 들어 주시고 재치 있는 농담도 해 주시며 격려와 응원에 늘 많은 도움을 얻었습니다. 감사합니다.

Sam: I'd like to say thank you that you always supported and gave a lot of encouragement genuinely. You always listened to everything that I was worried about like a real sister would sincerely and shared many witty jokes with me. I felt a lot of comfort from you. Thank you!

> * genuinely - 진정으로, 순수하게
> * sincerely – 진심으로
> * witty - 재치 있는

* 같은 내용의 다른 문장
Sam: You were someone I knew I could always turn to when something was bothering me. Through all of this, you gave me so much support, more than I could have ever asked for from you. Everything you ever gave me, your encouragement, your willing-ears, your support, I know all of it came sincerely. You have always listened to all of my worries and pains without judging me for what I have to say. Telling me witty jokes just to see me smile brought me so much comfort. I don't feel that I've said this to you enough times—thank you!

> * turn to – 의지하다
> * willing-ears – 다른 사람 말을 잘 들어주는
> * sincerely – 진심으로
> * I don't feel that I've said this to you enough times. – 이 말을 충분히 못한 것 같다.

Eunice: 늘 긍정적인 생각과 다른 사람을 돕고 싶은 진심 어린 마음, 그 안에서의 큰 에너지로 인생을 더 밝은 방향으로 바라볼 수 있게 해주신 저의 스승! Eunice 언니!

언니 정말로 언니의 존재만으로도 너무 감사해요.
언니의 미국 의사 과정을 누구보다 열심히 응원하겠습니다.
저와의 좋은 추억들 만들어 주셔서 너무 감사하고 많은 철없는 행동들 다 받아 주심에 다시 한번 감사합니다!

Eunice: You were the one who always made me focus on my positive thoughts and the sincere desire to help others. Thank you for showing me how to see life in a brighter way.
You are one of my mentors; I'm really just thankful for your existence.
I will always be rooting for your success in becoming a doctor in the States more than anyone else. Thank you so much for making a lot of good memories with me.
Thank you for putting up with me through all these times again!

* desire – _____ (위에서 답 찾아보기)
* existence - 존재
* put up with – 참고 견디다
* through all these times – (과거의) 모든 지난날들을

* **같은 내용의 다른 문장**

Eunice: You are my teacher, sister and a mentor who always helped me to see the brighter side of things. You have a sincere desire to help others, and for me, that was seeing past my negative thoughts. I do not know how I would have continued without you to help me see that my future was not as bleak as it appeared in one of the most uncertain times in my life. You are one of my mentors who helped shape me, and I am ever so grateful that you found your way into my life. I will always be rooting for your success in becoming a doctor in the States more than anyone else. Thank you for creating so many good memories with me. Thank you for looking past my immature behavior and investing your time in helping me grow.

- * appear – 나타나다
- * root for someone – 누군가를 응원하다
- * continue without you – 당신 없이 계속하다
- * look past something – 무엇을 덮어주다, 모른 척해 주다, 넘어가 주다
- * see past something – 과거에 얽매어 있지 말고 앞을 내다보아라
- * bleak – 암울한, 미래가 없어 보이는
- * as bleak as it appeared – 암울하게만 보이는
- * one of the most uncertain times – 누군가의 불확실한 시간들
- * shape – 형성하다

캐나다인 Samantha Mudiappahpiilai
강인함 속에서 나오는 따뜻함을 가진 Samantha 언니, 늘 누군가를 위해 헌신하며 진심으로 사람들을 대해 주는 언니를 보며 캐나다에 진정한 천사가 아닐까, 라는 생각을 했습니다.
누구보다 진정으로 이야기 들어주고 따뜻한 이야기를 나눠 주며 좋은 사람으로 남아 주셔서 감사합니다. 늘 언니의 작은 천사들과 함께 좋은 일들만 있기를 기도하겠습니다.

Samantha, who has both warmth and strength, who is always devoted, treats people sincerely, and I truly thought you were a true angel from Canada.
Thank you for always listening to me sincerely, sharing warm stories, and remaining as a good influence. I will always pray that only good things will happen to your little angels and your family.

- * warmth – 온기, 따뜻함
- * strength – 힘, 용기
- * devote – 바치다, 쏟다
- * treat – 대하다
- * remain – 남다
- * pray – 기도하다

* **같은 내용의 다른 문장**

Samantha: Your strength lies in the warmth you give others. You are a good person who always devotes time and energy in treating others sincerely. I thought you were an angel during my time in Canada. You truly made me feel welcome during my time there.
Thank you for always listening to me, telling me stories about your life, and staying a good person unaltered by the world.
I will always pray for your success and that only good things happen to you and your little angels.

> * something lies in something – (무엇이) 어딘가 안에 내재되어 있다.
> * welcoming – 따뜻이 맞이하는
> * unaltered by the world - 세상에 때 묻지 않은(시적으로)
> * unaltered – 바뀌지 않은, 변하지 않은

뉴질랜드 언니 Leah-renei taurna: 사랑이 넘치는 뉴질랜드의 엉뚱 발랄한 Leah!
모든 걸 다 아낌없이 퍼 주면서도 아까워하지 않는 언니를 보며 순수한 사랑이라는 것이 무엇인지 많이 배울 수 있었습니다. 언니의 배려와 자비로운 사랑을 통해서 뉴질랜드 사람들의 문화와 사랑에 대해 배울 수 있게 해주어 너무 감사합니다. 우리 Leah 언니의 멋진 아들 Kira도 항상 건강하게 언니 옆을 지켜줄 수 있게 기도할게요. 사랑합니다.

My sister from New Zealand, Leah! You are such a bubbly and cheerful woman with full of love! I was able to learn what the genuine and true love was through seeing your willingness to be generous towards your friends and me whenever and wherever.
Thank you so much for allowing me to learn about your culture and love of Kiwis through your empathetic and merciful nature. Also, I will keep you and Kira in my prayers for your well-beings. I love you.

* bubbly – 쾌활한, 밝은
* cheerful – 밝은, 활기찬, 명랑한
* full of love – 사랑으로 가득한
* genuine – 진솔한
* willingness – 무엇을 할 의지
* generous - 베풀 줄 아는
* whenever and wherever – 언제 어디서든
* allow – 허락하다
* Kiwi – 뉴질랜드 사람(슬랭)
* empathetic – 공감할 수 있는 능력이 있는
* merciful nature - 자비로움 (그런 면이 있는)
* prayers – 기도
* well- being – 건강함, 안부

* 같은 내용의 다른 문장

Leah, my wonderful sister from the land of Lord of the Rings!
You are such a joy to be around with all your bubbliness and positive attitude!
I learned the true meaning of what it means to love and care for those around you through watching you being ever so generous towards your friends.
Thank you so much for taking me on a tour to observe your culture and loving nature of Kiwis through the loving lens within you.
Lastly, I will always keep you and Kira in my prayers for your fortunes. I love you.

* Lord of the Rings - 반지의 제왕
* bubbliness – 쾌활함, 밝음
* positive attitude – 긍정적인 태도
* observe – 관찰하다
* loving nature - 사랑을 하는 면모
* through the loving lens within you – 사랑을 하는 면이 가득한 너를 통해서

해외에서 가족같이 따뜻하게 대해 주었던 나의 뉴질랜드 친구 Pip Weird, Kelly Nepe, 영국인 Rawni Mayhew, 호주인 Larrissa Millard, Kat Ray Watson, Danny Weir 마지막으로 필리핀인 Rodelyn Mole 등 나의 인생에서 내가 한 단계 한 단계 성장하며 좋은 영향력을 나눠 주며 나의 20대 초중반에 큰 힘이 되어 준 것에 깊은 감사를 표하고 싶습니다.

To all whom have treated me as if I was one of their own, my dear friends Pip Weird and Kelly Nepe from New Zealand, Rawni Mayhew from UK, Larrissa Millard, Kat Ray Watson, and Danny Weir from Australia, and lastly Rodelyn Mole from Philippines; You guys all have shown me the way to become something better than I was before in my 20's by injecting me with strengths when I needed them, and for that, I sincerely want to thank you all from the bottom of my heart.

* injecting me with strengths – 힘을 불어넣어 주다
* from the bottom of my heart – 진심으로

* 같은 내용의 다른 문장

To all whom have treated me as if I was one of their own, my dear friends Pip Weird and Kelly Nepe from New Zealand, Rawni Mayhew from UK, Larrissa Millard, Kat Ray Watson, and Danny Weir from Australia, and lastly Rodelyn Mole from Philippines; Who were like my second family during my time abroad. All of you played a great part in influencing my life during my early-to-mid 20's. I would like to thank all of you sincerely.

"세상에 이런 영어를 가르치다니, 이런 표현을 쓰다니, 하고 감격하게" 만드는 빠다영어 캘리포니아 교포 Jay 선생님 저의 인생의 큰 디딤돌, 큰 계단이 되어 주시고 늘 지지하고 좋은 말, 가끔은 뼈 때리는 말들을 해 주셔서 감사합니다. 선생님 없는 저는 상상할 수도 없네요.

You are one of the teachers who has made me think, "I can't believe

there is an English teacher like him.... He is amazing!"
Teacher at "Buttery Smooth English" from California,
I'd like to say thank you so much for providing me with the stepping stone in my life and always supporting me and giving good advice. Although you are sometimes blunt, I can't imagine being myself without you! I really appreciate your sincere help.

> * stepping stone – _____ (위에서 답 찾아보기)
> * blunt – 직설적인
> * appreciate – 감사히 여기다
> * sincere help – 진심 어린 도움

* **같은 내용의 다른 문장**

You are one of the few teachers who have made me think, "I can't believe there is an English teacher like him. He is amazing! Teacher at "Buttery Smooth English" from California.
I want to say thank you so much for being a significant contributor in my life by always supporting me and encouraging me. Although sometimes you are rather blunt, even still, I can't imagine being myself without you! I really appreciate your sincere help!

> * significant – 중요한, 큰 의미가 있는
> * contributor – 기여자 (도움을 주는 사람)
> * encourage – 격려하다, 용기를 북돋우다

많은 사랑을 받고 있는 유튜브 구독자 40만 명, Aran English에 에듀테이너 김아란 선생님 많은 이들에게 늘 사랑과 격려 좋은 영향력을 나눠 주려는 그 열정과 사랑 늘 배우며 좋은 영향받으며 같이 성장하고 싶습니다.

Aran Kim, an 'edu-tainer' at Aran English who has 400,000 YouTube subscribers that is loved by many people, you are one of my mentors who has influenced me greatly.
I'd like to grow with you who always try to give good influence,

encouragement and love to others.

* subscriber – 구독자
* influence - 영향을 미치다
* greatly – 대단히, 크게

* 같은 내용의 다른 문장

* adore – 아주 좋아하다, 흠모하다
* be willing to – _____ (위에서 답 찾아보기)

Aran Kim, you have influenced me for quite a while now. As an 'edu-tainer' at Aran English with 400,000 YouTube subscribers who adore your channel, I'd like to grow with you. You always influence others, offer motivation, and offer your sincerity. It is my goal to be an 'edu-tainer' like yourself, who is so willing to share her passion and love with those around you.

라이프 코칭 멘토이자 늘 성장을 위해, 다른 사람들에게 큰 도움이 되고자 항상 노력하는 시카고 교포 Sharonkilonhan! 당신을 만나 라이프 코칭을 통해 많은 변화를 얻고 알게 됨에 너무 영광이었고 큰 영감을 주셔서 감사합니다.

Sharon Kilonhan from Chicago is a life-coaching mentor, a warm person who always tries to be helpful to others and be part of peoples' lives. It was such an honor to meet you and thank you for your great inspiration; I was able to change myself with your life coachings a lot!

* 같은 내용의 다른 문장
A life-coaching mentor, a warm individual who always goes that extra mile to help others and be an important part of people's lives, I want to thank you, Sharon Kilonhan from Chicago.
Every time I take your program, it really motivates and helps me to

get inspired.
Thank you for all the hard work that you dedicate to others.

> * life-coaching – 인생 상담 코치(개인의 생활과 일에 대한 조언을 해 주도록 고용된 사람)
> * individual - 개인, 개성 있는 사람
> * go extra mile to - ~동사 위해 특별히 애를 쓰다
> * inspire – 영감을 주다
> * dedicate – _____ (위에서 답 찾아보기)

그저 나의 학생, 가족들에게 큰 힘이 되고 싶고 성장하고 싶다는 《찐 미국사람 영어회화》의 저자 Lora 교포 선생님, 선생님의 밝고 강한 에너지 지금처럼 뿌려 나가며 세상을 밝게 비추어 나갔으면 좋겠습니다. J

You have said that you want to be a good teacher and a comfort to your students and grow together. Lora, an author who wrote Real American English Conversation, I hope you continue to spread your bright and positive energy to brighten the world as you hope.

> * comfort – _____ (위에서 답 찾아보기)
> * author – 저자
> * continue – 계속하다
> * spread – 퍼뜨리다
> * brighten – 밝히다

＊ 같은 내용의 다른 문장
Lora, an author who wrote "Real American English Conversation", I hope that you continue to spread your positive energy in the learning community to brighten the world together.

> * brighten – (분위기, 더 나은 세상을) 만들다, 밝히다

마지막으로 너무 부족한 딸이지만 키워주시고 많은 것들에 도움을 주신 부모님께 감사드립니다.

Lastly, I would like to thank my parents for raising me and helping me with many things, even though I am a daughter who is lacking so much.

* lack - ~이 없다, 부족하다

* **같은 내용의 다른 문장**
Lastly, I would like to thank my parents for raising me and helping me with many things even though I am a daughter who is lacking so much. Thank you for everything you have given me throughout my life, such as your love, the hope you instilled in me, and now the bright future.

* instilled – ~에 심어 놓은
* the hope you instilled in me - 내 안에 심어놓은 희망
* throughout - ~동안 쭉, 내내

아직 먼 길을 가야 하지만 그 안에서 늘 든든한 지원이 되어주신 많은 선생님들과 친구, 가족 사랑하고 늘 큰 은혜 잊지 않고 나아가겠습니다. 사랑합니다.

I still have a long way to go, but I love the teachers, friends, and family members who have always been a strong support for me. And, I will always continue to keep moving forward and I will always keep your support in my heart with gratitude. I love you.
I still have a long way to go. The journey of life is a long one, but the love my teachers, friends, and family members have given me along the way will keep me on course. No matter where you are, all of you will be a constant reminder of all the love and support I have gained over the years. It will be enough to keep me going for the rest of my life. Remembering our time together fills me with happiness. I will never be able to truly express. Again, thank you, and I love each of

you for coming into my life when I needed you the most.

* have a long way to go - 아직 멀었다, 갈 길이 멀다
* journey of life - 삶의 여정
* keep me on course - 옳은 길을 갈 수 있게끔 하다
* constant reminder – 지속적으로 되뇌게 해주는 것
* I have gained over the years. – 시간이 지나며 무엇을 얻었다.

VI

영어를 배우려면 이분들과 이런 기능들을 이용하자!

영어를 배우려면 이분들과 이런 기능들을 이용하자!

저자의 추천 한국 YouTuber들

Aran TV

YouTube 구독자 40만 명을 보유하고 있으며, 한국인이 알기 쉽지 않은 영어 표현들뿐만 아니라 외국 문화, 자기 계발, 신앙 관련 다양한 영상들을 올려주시고 계신다.

아란 샘은 YouTube 뿐 아니라 자체 홈페이지를 개설하여 에듀테이너, 아름답고 찬란한 인생 학교 교장 선생님으로서, 큰 꿈을 품고 선한 영향을 나누고자 하시는 목표로, 사람들에게 좋은 도움이 될 만한 활동들을 열어 주시고 계신다. Instagram이나 YouTube 채널을 한번 확인해 보자. 분명 내가 왜 이 채널을 이제 알았지? 하고 신이 날 것이다.

https://www.youtube.com/channel/UCmoUsPP4mD9-PPdRmeUI05A

날라리 데이브

유튜브 구독자 18만 명의 유튜버!
미국 교포이며 한국어와 영어 모든 완벽하다 싶을 정도로 언어 구사력이 매우 뛰어나신 영기 샘! 닉네임과 같이 영상 안에 영어, 미국 문화, 뉴스, 연애상담 등을 유튜브와 블로그 등 다양한 주제로 활동 중이시다.
날라리 데이브 님의 브이로그를 통해 찐 영어를 배울 수 있다.

https://www.youtube.com/channel/UCLub64OvZbs6aGj_qJnuWKw/videos

로라 TV

인스타 팔로워 3만 명, 유튜브 구독자 8천 명 이상을 보유하고 있는 전 대형 유명 어학원 강사, 적을 수 없이 많은 영어 관련 경력들로 바쁘게 활동 중이신 캘리포니아 교포 로라 샘! 한국, 영어 목소리 둘 다 너무 멋지게 구사할 줄 아시는 영어 강사님. 인스타, 유튜브뿐만 아니라 조금만 검색하면 요즘 유명한 웬만한 영어 관련 앱, 강의에서 만나볼 수 있다.

https://youtube.com/c/KimLora

Bridge TV

유튜브 15만 명을 소유하고 계신 태훈 샘.
한국에서 자라서 한국 외국어대학교를 졸업하셨는데도 불구하고 원어민들도 놀랄 만한 영어를 구사하시며 발음, 고급 영어, 시사 영어 등으로 한국인들이 모를 만한 학습법들을 핵심적인 표현, 발음들을 유튜브, 인스타, 틱톡, 클럽하우스 등으로 알려주시며 많은 영어 사업을 진행하시고 계신 능력자 태훈 샘! 영상 하나만 봐도 이 사람이 한국에서만 진짜 공부한 사람이 맞나? 싶을 정도이니 한번 유튜브 영상이나 검색해서 찾아보자!
https://www.youtube.com/c/BridgeTVKorea/videos

선민_sunmin

구독자 32만 명의 유튜버! 외국 팝송을 가사뿐만 아니라 문화, 배경지식 등을 설명하며 노래까지 부르며 설명을 해 주신다.
영어는 단어, 문법, 표현뿐 아니라 문화를 배우는 것도 공부 중 하나다.
아름다운 목소리로 엉뚱한 매력을 가지신 선민님의 유튜브에 들어가서 신나는 노래도 듣고 영어도 듣고 선민님의 엉뚱한 매력에 빠져 보길 바란다.
https://www.youtube.com/c/SunminJeong

오픽노잼

YouTube 구독자 22만 명의 오픽 시험 대비를 도와주시는 오픽 전문 영어 선생님. 캐나다에서 대학까지 졸업하시고 영어 관련 사업과 《오픽노잼》이라는 오픽 시험 준비 책도 출간하신 오픽 노잼 샘 시험이 아니어도 정말 이게 시험을 위한 영상이 맞나 싶을 정도로 재치 있게 재미있고 웃긴 표현들을 많이 알려주시는 강사님 특히 오픽을 준비한다면 모르는 사람이 없을 정도다. 시험이 아니라도 영상을 보면 오픽을 준비하고 싶어질지도 모른다.

영어 강사 Anna(hi_anna_ssam)

전 대형 학원 인기 강사 경력을 가지고 계시며, 인스타 팔로워 1.3만을 보유하고 있는 Anna 샘.
문법, 영어 다양한 표현들을 만화, 영상 등으로 아주 재치 있고 웃기게 편집해서 올려 주신다.
인스타 스토리 며칠만 보아도 영어 코미디언 강사가 있으면 이 선생님이지 않을까 하는 생각을 주게 해 주시는 강사님. 영어를 두려움 없이 편하고 재미있게 다가갈 수 있게 만들어 주는 강사님 인스타 팔로우를 하면 다양한 자료, 책, 강의들을 찾아볼 수 있다.

저자의 추천 해외 YouTuber들

Speak English with Vanessa
미국인이 가르쳐 주는 찐 영어 표현, 속담, 발음(구독자 370만 명)

Tina yong
호주에 살 고 있는 메이크업 유튜버(구독자 350만 명)

Liza Koshy
유학시절 많은 외국인 친구들이 추천해 준 코믹한 내용으로 미국 문화, 삶, 유행들을 알 수 있는 채널 (구독자 1750만 명)

Trevor Wallance
코믹 &욕 &문화 (구독자 240만 명)

Jenn im
한국인 부모님에서 태어난 미국 교포 패션, 브이로그, 문화(구독자 320만 명)

Babish Culinary University
다양한 나라 요리 음식 요리법을 알려주는 채널(950만 명)

First we Feast
전 세계 다양한 음식과 소스들 등 엽기적이고 재미있는 영상을 선보이는 채널 (1100만 명)

매우 유용한 영어 관련 애플리케이션

Italkl, Preply
– 전 세계 원어민들을 통해 아주 다양한 언어를 배울 수 있는 과외 애플리케이션이다.
영어뿐만 아니라 150개 국어 이상의 언어를 많은 전문가들이 적게는 시간당 5천 원 많게는 8만 원 이상을 받고 수업을 해 주고 있다. 나에게 맞는 시간, 맞는 가격, 맞는 선생님을 골라서 온라인으로 수업을 들을 수 있다.

Udemy
183,000개 이상의 강의와 4천만 명 이상의 수강생이 있는 온라인 학습 및 교수 마켓플레이스이다. 영어뿐 아니라 프로그래밍, 마케팅, 데이터 과학 및 그 밖의 분야에 대해 배워 볼 수 있으며 원어민들도 영어로 다양한 작문, 심리학 자기가 관심 있는 수업을 어느 정도 비용을 내고 수업을 듣는 애플리케이션이다.

Meet up
외국에서 뿐만 아니라 우리나라에서도 쓰이고 있는 웹 사이트, 애플리케이션. 우리나라 소모임 애플리케이션이라고 보면 된다. 다양한 취미, 모임들을 검색하여 우리나라에 있는 외국인들과 함께 다양한 활동을 할 수 있다.